Inner Journey

Inner
Journey

Inner Journey

Awake Today, Live Tomorrow

LORRAINE TRICKSEY

Matador
Unit E2 Airfield Business Park
Harrison Road, Market Harborough
Leicestershire LE16 7UL
Tel: 0116 279 2299
Email: books@troubador.co.uk
Web: www.troubador.co.uk/matador
Twitter: @matadorbooks

ISBN 978 1803137 476

British Library Cataloguing in Publication Data.
A catalogue record for this book is available from the British Library.

Printed and bound in the UK by TJ Books Limited, Padstow, Cornwall
Typeset in 11pt Minion Pro by Troubador Publishing Ltd, Leicester, UK

Matador is an imprint of Troubador Publishing Ltd

This book is dedicated with love to my husband Matt and
our children
Lyndsey, Charlene, Lewis, Pettina, Tiffiny, Ashley, and
Bethany –
because they fill my heart with joy.

Acknowledgements

I would like to give gratitude to my husband Matt for his devoted love, companionship, and support throughout our 41 years of marriage. To my children, for choosing me to be their mum and for just being themselves. Also, my lovely dad, for his guidance throughout my life, and to my mum for all the deep lessons she provided for my soul to grow.

I add a big heartfelt thank you to Tracy Willoughby, for sharing her knowledge and wisdom in helping me get started on writing this book, supporting me throughout my writing journey and helping me get it to print, but mostly for helping me make my dream come true.

About Me

Hello, my name is Lorraine Tricksey. I am first a wife and mum to 7 beloved children including a spirit son. I am also a gran to 15 cherished grandchildren.

I work as a full-time mum, wife, Medium, and healer-

As a spiritual teacher I have over 30 years' experience, as well as a lifetime interest in the spirit world and the meaning of life, which became heightened after the loss of our young son Lewis. However, from this life changing event many doors started to open and what followed enhanced a passion of helping others with the help and communications from my guide and spirit son. These lifetime teachings I now share with all those that are drawn to read this book.

I qualified with the Dorset Hants and Wiltshire Spiritual Association in spiritual healing. I am a Reiki Master and teacher, crystal therapist, and intuitively read the tarot, and am a qualified palm reader. I also hold meditation and spiritual development circles and earth ceremonies.

Together with my husband Matt we founded 'The Healing Garden Centre,' a spiritual place that brought together herbaceous plants, animals, and the spiritual world. This is also the home of 'Hocus Pocus.' where we sell high quality crystals and share knowledge from these special gems.

If you feel drawn to find out more there are contact details at the end of this book.

Introduction

I had been aware of the ticking from the old vintage school clock all day.

It was absolutely pouring with rain. As I ran home, I could feel the cold spray from the sodden paths splashing up my legs as it hit, just above my white school socks. My long blonde hair dripped as it hung plastered to my head and face, like I had just stepped out from the shower, but I knew the cut through route like the back of my hand. The unused and mostly overgrown pathway I took to get home quickly to see a very special lady.

I was always in awe of my gran, not only for the love and commitment she constantly showed her ever growing family, but for the wisdom she shared. She held our large family together and could always see the way through everyone's problems. I didn't realise back then, that she too had the spiritual gift, which I was to find out later, ran through my mum's family.

I remember often thinking...

'When I'm older I want to be as wise as my gran.'

In my work today, the wise old ways are very important. I always go back to old wisdoms with the help and guidance of my guides, who lead me to using my spiritual abilities to help clients with their emotions, illnesses, stresses, and everyday problems. They have shown me how the old wisdoms have been lost and forgotten over time and need to be rediscovered, with people becoming far more in tune with their own lives, hearts, bodies, earth cycles and the natural ways of being.

I am writing the memories of my earliest spiritual experiences as my guides remind me. They may not necessarily be in the correct order, but it is how they have been channelled through.

There have been situations throughout my own life that have evoked strong emotions for me to learn from. Over time my guides have shown different spiritual learnings to help me understand, deal with, and heal.

From these great teachings, I am now able to help others. I will say throughout all my life's lessons, I have always felt extremely loved and have also tried to work through them all from my own heart with love.

'We can never truly walk in another man's shoes
until we have trodden the same pathway ourselves.'

This book is my story, my teachings, learnings, and experiences. It is written with hope, to pass on spiritual wisdoms, to help enlighten people and make their pathways easier for them to tread. There may be situations that replicate some in your own life, and the lessons learned from them may help you move forward from fears or blocks attached. Others you read may not resonate with you at this moment in time, but may be recalled sometime later to help family, friends, and people around you.

I hope you enjoy reading this book as much as I have channelling and writing it for whoever is guided to read it.

I will add if you are reading my book it will be for a reason with something you need to learn.

'Spiritual wisdoms need to be learnt and shared.'

My Journey

There was excitement and anticipation in the air, as I sat in the garden waiting for my dear dad to come and join me, looking up, far and wide into the soft blue, summer sky, waiting for his pigeons to return home. I loved spending time with him, I was quite a daddy's girl. I even remember walking down the street, trying to copy his large steps, which was quite hard with my then small legs. I have always had a natural yearning to be close to my dad, but it wasn't until I was a lot older, and my guides started to show me the dynamics in my family, I realised why I viewed this bond as so special.

As a child, I couldn't have changed a thing. It was only necessary to live through the experiences coping and reacting as only a child would. Sometimes naivety and innocence, is a blessing in itself. We don't need to see the bigger picture at that time. Just experiences, which create emotions, for us to learn from at some point in our lives. All of this helps create the person we are to become.

It was a Saturday afternoon and pigeon racing day. The

homing birds had already been taken to their destination by a driver from the local racing club.

It was nearly time for the birds to arrive home. The spotting, calling in of the birds, removal of their rubber ring, identification tags and placing in the pigeon racing clock was an art itself. Every second counted to clock in the winning time. Dad was an expert at this and knew his birds like the back of his hand, spotting them at quite a distance. He would often return home from the local club with rosettes and cups, quietly proud of himself. I always called my dad the bird man as he cared for different types most of his life and had an innate understanding of them. He taught me so much about the natural way of looking after and understanding animals, which I use in my animal healings and communication teachings today. Animals also teach us so much about our own lives.

'I have always felt very protected and never alone.'

However, one of these Saturday afternoons was different. I had gone out into the garden a little early and was sitting on the wooden bench, leaning back looking into the sky whilst listening to the songbirds singing and watching them feed from the overflowing bird table. I was lost in my own thoughts when I had an overwhelming feeling around me. I didn't feel frightened, but almost as though I was being watched or someone was very close. As soon as it had happened, it disappeared. It was the same feeling but much stronger, I used to get in my bedroom at night when all was quiet. Something I would learn to understand far more when I was older. These were the first early communication signs from my *Native American Guide* letting me know he was around to guide and protect me.

> '*When your mind is quiet it is easier
> for guides to connect with you.*'

Years later, when sat in deep meditation, the energy around me began to change quite noticeably and I felt as though I was physically growing. At the same time, through my third eye, I saw a Native American in full ceremonial costume. He introduced himself as my guide. This was the same feeling, but much larger and stronger than I had experienced when I was younger. The time was right for my guide to introduce himself properly and for our connection to become stronger, as he was now ready to work with me and I was at the right stage in my life for this to happen.

We are all as individual as fingerprints and have our own life journeys, filled with lessons to be experienced which helps our souls grow to become more enlightened. Our development will be in our own time and unique way.

I believe from my guide's teachings, that before we reincarnate, our higher selves choose Spiritual Guides. They help us fulfil our own spiritual contract, for our soul's learnings in this lifetime.

We have guides that stay alongside us for the entire incarnation. They also evolve, through their commitment and sharing of our experiences. Others appear at certain times, helping with different areas and lessons in our lives. Some are highly ascended Masters, whilst others less evolved come in with their expertise in certain fields when needed. They can occasionally be deceased family members. My grandad, who passed when I was about 5 years of age, came through to help me, with a significant part of my life, which I will share with you later in my book.

Many guides, but not all, would have at some time in their evolution trodden the earth plane, whilst others would have never had physical form.

Our guides use our energy fields and spiritual gifts to connect with us. It can come via a gut feeling, a sense of knowing, when really you don't, but the feeling is so strong, it can't be ignored and usually turns out right. We can even see visions in our third eye or hear a voice spoken that isn't our own.

These psychic abilities are clairvoyance which means clear knowing, clairaudience to hear those in the spirit world, clairsentience is sensing exactly how another is feeling and the energies around. Mediums are those who see spirit and are born with the gift, it cannot be developed, but the psychic can.

- Life is a great teacher -

My guide has always shown me, we choose our parents, brothers, sisters, family etc., and two or three emotions we can learn from, before we reincarnate back onto the earth plane, to help us with karma and our soul's growth. These emotions will be repeated throughout our lifetime in different ways, until we have learnt the lessons attached to them.

I often hear students and clients say, 'but I have already dealt with my past,' or 'I have walked away from it.' This was something I also did, on quite a few occasions, but I was always gently guided back, as there were unfinished lessons for me to learn. Everything is, however, personal choice and when progressing through our life's teachings, it can be like peeling off the layers of an onion. As we learn and grow, our vibrational energy changes and the next layer will then be shown to us. However, it will be viewed and dealt with differently each time, as we would have changed, from when it was visited before. Eventually, we will have expanded our consciousness, grown from our experiences and they will not hurt or affect us anymore. On reflection, they may have felt very painful or hard. However, on viewing from a higher perspective, we will thank them for the soul growth they have provided in helping shape the person we are. This can sometimes be hard to see at the time of the event and can only truly be appreciated on reflection.

It is easy to walk away from people you find difficult, that your vibration attracted, but I believe new friends, will teach similar lessons time and time again, until you have learnt what life is trying to show you.

With family, through my life's experiences and my guide's guidance, I have been shown it can be different. You just can't break the connection and often we wouldn't want to. However, believe me, at times I have really tried. Even if you don't see those closely related or have been adopted there is always a connection. It may be in your mind, heart or simply a pulling or searching feeling, you just can't get rid of. However, if you have family difficulties, sometimes it is one parent you find challenging, it can be good to journey back through their life and try to understand where the traits have come from.

Why do they act this way? Often a bullying or domineering father would have been treated the same by their dad and so he is imitating past behaviours. It may be in his learning, to change this pattern, not pass it to the next generation. This is often where timeline healing can be very useful. However, with the laws of karma, it could be linked to a past life. For instance, if you were once a bully, this time you could find yourself the victim, being shown its effects to help serve any past karma.

I have written below an example based on my experiences of working with different people in my healing practice. This illustrates to you how an emotion can be presented in different ways, throughout a young person's lifetime, which was held until she learnt the lessons attached…

Here are some examples…

At approximately five or six years of age, their dad left the family home. As a child, they wouldn't have been able to do much about this, apart from maybe rely on mum for survival and live through the experience. However, on some level in their consciousness they would have felt the emotional effects of masculine detachment.

Later in their life, a friend could have left for another school, in teenage years a partner ended their relationship, later their marriage eventually ended in divorce whilst their children were still young (repeated pattern) and future love relationships fell apart for one reason or another.

All of these examples show detachment of male energy in their life and highlight the same emotion, but in a different way each time. Consequently, any future partners they choose, could have the same vibrational energy, as the dad they are trying to replace and never stayed the course, to fulfil the emotions they haven't dealt with and fill the void in their heart.

The accumulation of all these events would have undoubtedly left the person with very low self-moral.

Some people feel it important to have a partner in their lives, to distinguish their identity and enhance themselves. However, when one spends time alone and stops searching for a relationship, it can present a time of reflection and the discovery of one's true self, by visiting their own silent thoughts, coping with life, surviving, and possibly facing their own fear of being alone.

Our anxieties and fears can be our biggest gifts. If we embrace them, the lessons attached help make us stronger, if we are afraid and don't face them, they hold us week. If anything in life makes you fearful always find a way of meeting it, to set yourself free and grow.

Personal development can give great life tools, building of character and enhancement of self-love can start to shine through, especially if they retract the love they were constantly giving away, back to themselves.

It is often when people are at their lowest and feeling as though they have hit a brick wall in life (which is actually a valuable place to be) when they search for help and find themselves guided to my door. A time where we journey back with healing and help, from my spirit guides to the route cause and its affects.

As a consequence of the lady's experiences, I gave an example of earlier, her aura will hold the vibrational energy from the emotions, thoughts, and feelings she encountered from these past difficult times and will act as a mirror to attract future partners to her, from the energy it reflects to the outside world. So, if she is showing the expression of a victim, she could attract someone with a strong vibrational energy, as that is the energy her soul requires on an unconscious level, to develop and grow. The universe always provides what we need, not necessarily what we feel we require. So, the strong partner at first would give her the strength she craves but can also enhance her weaknesses. If she recognises this and looks at what life is trying to teach her, she will take steps to become emotionally strong by changing her reactions and let go of the victim mode. When we recognise our actions are not benefiting ourselves, we can start to make changes. At first it can go well, but then we see ourselves reverting to old ways. This is still not bad so long as we correct them again. Similar, to making a mistake when learning something. It is often good to get something wrong as we learn from the process and remember the right way next time. When we make changes to our reactions to situations that have hurt us, our auric field will alter and attract different to us. The old ways will no longer feel right.

Another way I have seen this type of situation evolve referring back to my example of the lady, is whilst she is emitting a vibration of needing to be rescued, feeling vulnerable, desperate for love, she could attract men who are looking for victims, so to speak, who will play to their male ego, through their own desperation for love. Sometimes these men have had problems with their mum, or other females close to them and don't quite know where to put their own love, so they try here and there. In fact, any women that shows them affection will do, to temporarily fulfil their hearts desire, which was broken usually in childhood. In a sense they could be mirroring the ladies they attract. They are trying to fulfil the loss of special female energy and the lady is trying to replace the detached love of the male she lost, who didn't stay the course as he had his own problems and was forever searching for lost love. So, as you can now see, from wanting her dad's love, she is attracting in males with the same vibrational energy as dad, so chances are they also won't stay long term. It sounds complicated but it is simple when considered.

I always recommend stopping at this point, to work on oneself with a good healer, to settle any emotional disturbances in the auric field, balance chakras, and learn techniques for self-love and thus change what they are reflecting out from their aura.

If you remember me saying like attracts like, so we really need to be giving out what we want to attract in and if we are coming from an **unbalanced** perspective, it can be very hard. Also, when vibrational energy is changed, one's whole persona can feel lighter, enabling fears to be faced and stagnant emotions and situations to be dealt with, confidence and energy levels enhanced and once more embracing life. What is then attracted in will be different, be it people, situations, love, money, happiness etc, always positive changes.

'Be a reflection, of what you want.
If you want love – give love (especially to yourself)
If you want respect – be respectful to yourself
and the world around you.
If you want honesty – be honest to yourself
and everything you do.'

Just as a point of interest whilst explaining this, I often find clients who come to me for healing, who are dealing with childhood issues relating to their fathers, often end up having mostly male children. As they have come back to learn about male energy, which can be shown through their grandads, dad, brothers, sons, and if they have still not learnt, from their grandsons. This is what I call timeline teachings, when situations and attached emotions will repeat with subsequent family members until the lessons have been experienced, understood, and learnt from.

They could also find themselves facing responsibility, authority, hard work and commitment. Any imbalances in their auric field, aches, pains, illnesses and so on, will often be found on the right-hand side of their body. These can show up at any times in their lives and are usually linked to karma they need to work through.

However, it will be visa-versa when there has been a problem with their mum. It will be the left-hand side of the body which influences and shows any imbalances. They will probably have more female figures in their lives, such as substitute mums, who have turned up just at the right time to support them through difficult times. Sometimes acting as a surrogate to give them love, nurturing or even guidance at their times of need. Female energy guides us to connect with the feminine, encourages going with the flow of life, females are the doers who get things done and reflect creativity, also homemakers and balance in life.

At a recent workshop there was a lovely lady who attended, but I could sense she had experienced deep pain. I was pulled to her left eye which intuitively kept appearing to me as being sunken back and dark, whilst getting thoughts she had suffered deep pain where her mum was concerned. Much later in the day I heard her telling one of the other ladies how her mum had died when she was a young child.

So, can you see how our bodies reflect pains we are carrying? Our eyes illustrate how we view life and to be stepped back showed the loss she had experienced and not dealt with.

'The struggle you are in today
is developing the strengths you will need tomorrow.'

Energy healing such as Reiki, crystal, or spiritual healing can be a great aid to our everyday lives. It works by balancing out the chakras, any emotional disturbances in the auric field, and especially, helps to kick start the body into healing itself and encourage one onto their own personal journey of self-discovery, which often aids learning self-love.

You can truly trust your higher self and by learning to connect and trust it, maybe through meditation or with a good healer, will help you come from a much stronger perspective. It can change your momentum and personal strengths, helping you start to face any fears that have not been dealt with and are holding you back. Confidence levels can grow, changing your vibrational energy, with life being embraced and viewed differently, not turned away from. What we attract to ourselves, be it people, situations, love, money, happiness etc., will be different and positive changes can be experienced once again.

'In order to let go of any pains and burdens you have been carrying around with you, such as grief, self-destruction, self-loathing, and heartache, you need to first meet them, learn what they are showing you and respect their existence. For them to gift you, freedom, and a life as it really should be.'

Auras

Colourful, flashing disco lights created a wonderful ambience on every wall, whilst the band's music echoed, filling the hall with memorable songs of younger years, all sounding exceptionally good. The whole room felt alive.

So many people, many of them long term friends chatting and laughing, with the dance floor a hive of activity. Everyone doing their own thing and all the combined noises blending together, creating a constant buzz, which ricocheted around the room. So many greetings, happiness, fun and laughter in one area, so why the feeling of wanting to run away, coupled with a retraction of the energy field and solar plexus, combined with a feeling of needing to reciprocate with spoken words but quietness prevailing, with constant chatter in the head, mingling with a feeling of not belonging and sitting on the edge of everything that was happening?

A fun day planned spending quality time with beloved family, with money in the pocket, musing through shops looking for treasures to be had – but so many people – too many people. Didn't matter which way one turned or tried to walk there were people.

I am sure many of you have had this feeling, where your mind becomes clogged, as you try to walk around them. One after another they present in front of you. Legs aching, mind and body feeling heavy and any thoughts of purchasing becoming a distant memory, until the familiar feeling of wanting to leave returns – but why do you feel this way and others don't?

Have you ever walked into a room and suddenly felt agitated when you were previously relaxed? One day awoke with a spring in your step and another felt as though a brick was holding you down in bed or been drawn to wearing specific colours.

We have all had that favourite top we adore, with plans to wear to a certain place, party, or event. However, on the day with plans of your attire all in place, the top just doesn't look and sometimes even feel right, so, you change. Is it the colour, the style? often we really don't know, but one thing is for sure, it isn't the right outfit for the day.

That horrible feeling when you are in a room full of people but have a sense of not belonging. So, what is all this about?

As you know we all have a physical body, but not everyone recognises we also have an energetic field extending from it, which is called our Aura. It can have a big effect on our physical form. It is made up of several layers which are constantly changing depending on what we are experiencing – seeing, feeling, hearing, sensing etc, around us.

I will explain in more detail about the different layers a little bit later in this chapter. But for now, be aware of it.

Those who are sensitive to energy, can often have similar experiences to those I have written above. However, many are not aware of just how perceptive they are to the different vibrations around them and can sometimes start to feel isolated, or as though they are different from others who don't have the same feelings and a sense of not belonging or fitting in can prevail.

When you are in a room full of different people, they are all emitting their own frequencies of energy through their auric fields, depending on past experiences, and also, events currently happening in their lives. Some will pertain to be happy even if they are sad, but intuitively this can be seen through.

If someone is sensitive these energies can be picked up on and feel overwhelming, especially if one doesn't know how to protect their own auric field from them. Also, for those born a spirit medium, there can be constant chatter in their head from personal guides and the spirit world interacting with them, many can view this as their own thoughts, but by spiritually developing to understand their special gift, can start to decipher their own thinking from their spirit helper's messages. Spirit will link into our energy field to help bring the messages through. So, you can start to see why some mediums cannot tolerate a lot of noise because of the communications they are hearing.

My guide has always shown me that when the spirit world draws near, they don't see your physical appearances but are drawn to your vibrational light. So, loved ones in the spirit world recognise your energetic glow. The more developed one becomes the brighter their aura will be.

Sometimes others loved ones draw close to a medium

if they have messages to convey which aren't being heard. However, saying that a Medium shouldn't walk around open to spirit communications all the time, or they will drain their own energies. It is important to shut down one's spiritual connection when not working. If a message is imperative and needs to come through their guides and the spirit world will let them know.

I am sure you can recall walking into a place where you felt very at ease, comfortable, peaceful, possibly with feelings of having come home, even though you have never been there before? Or alternatively felt extremely uncomfortable, possibly fearful whilst looking for your escape route when there is no reason for these feelings.

As you walk through a crowd, enter a different space, room, office etc., that area will have retained different vibrational energies from the people, animals etc., who have been there and their interactions, so your auric field will pick up on this collective energy and you will respond accordingly, often on a subconscious level.

Have you ever experienced that retracted feeling of shrinking back within yourself, almost wanting to appear invisible or even smaller to divert attention? This is when you are pulling in your aura and is usually for protection, as it has sensed an incompatible energy or fear. Whilst another time, your heart chakra extends producing feelings of peace, calm and readiness to reach out to others – you are surrounded by compatible, enhancing energy.

Animal Auras

I have learnt so much from the animal kingdom who are very receptive with their own energetic field and the vibrations around them. They have kept their natural instincts alive using all their senses, which as we have become more westernised have forgotten.

If you observe a small dog out for a walk, sometimes you can see it lift its back leg right up, even stand on tip toe and urinate as high in a bush as it can many times along its route. It has sensed a much larger, energetically stronger animal in its vicinity and is trying to appear bigger than it is, an instinctive defence mechanism to protect its area and for survival of the strongest.

Animals' intuition keeps them very in tune with their bodies, so when their physical or auric field is out of balance they will automatically respond to realign it, often frequenting different energetic areas to enhance this. For example, if it needs peace after an active or aggressive time, it will rest in a calming vibrational area, such as a bed of Lavender or cats amongst the Nepeta mint. If they want to fight or need to build energy to protect their homes, offspring, or themselves, they may spend time for instance under a holly bush or a great oak to help create this vibration, especially if the soil was reddened. They may raise their energy levels by running around, then resting and repeating the process.

How many times have you seen an animal make a shallow in the ground and lay their tummies on the cool often damp soil? This action will not only ground their life force, but also help their emotional centre or whichever part of their body they present there. Chickens do this by creating dirt baths, but also if they have red mite, as it cools their aggravated bodies.

So, from my examples of the animals you can see just how important it is to keep our auric fields and physical bodies in balance and ground by simply sitting, laying down or ambling barefooted on grass, spending time in nature or going for a long walk.

Protection

I have clear memories of the familiar sound of the small gate clicking closed behind us, as we walked along the timeworn concrete path aligning a well-loved and neatly kept bed of beautiful cottage perennials and traditional scented roses, we would come to the well-known door, that was forever open to their family and friends.

Always greeted with a welcoming smile, the kettle boiling and an aroma of fresh washing wafting through the air.

Such fond memories of visiting my mother in laws home, where it was so relaxing you could feel every cell of your body let go, with the yearning for our home to feel the same way. This was never going to happen with six young lively children, their excitable energies and two businesses operating from it. Also, it wouldn't have been right, our home was exactly as it needed to be for each of us back then and the activities and experiences that needed to take place. However, it was lovely to visit my in-laws and take time out to unwind. Although now we are older, and life has changed our home has that familiar feeling and I can sense the same vibrational energy change when our lovely family visit.

My guide showed me a very simple technique which I like to teach to help others protect their auras and is quite easy, so anyone can do it. When you are in a place or with people that are incompatible with your own energy field and you start to feel out of sorts as your vibration doesn't fit with theirs or you are struggling in some way such as being in a busy shopping centre, depressed places, hospitals etc, you can simply create in your mind's eye a hooded cloak of protection all the way around yourself.

If I can ask you to just visualise for one moment – our auric fields can extend out quite far when we are happy and relaxed, so when in busy areas our energies are intermingling with those around us and will be picking up on the vibrations contained in other auras, without us consciously realising. However, by putting this technique I am going to show you in place, it can help create an energetic boundary so to speak around your auric field which can really help – why not try it to see?

So, what is a cloak of protection?

It is a way of focusing one's energy field with intention, into a way to protect oneself, creating a sacred space to journey on a soul's pathway with feelings of protection, help and upliftment and even assisting in expanding universal consciousness in any way their focus may take them. It's a thought!

My guide illustrated to me how the protective cloak is a sacred symbol, which when created mentally helps evoke a higher universal vibration to enhance a shield of safety surrounding the person whenever it is felt needed and called in.

So why would you want to protect your spiritual energy?

How many times have you been with someone only to come away feeling absolutely drained, and tired, or with negative thoughts replacing ideas of expansion and creativeness? Have you ever walked into a room and felt the negativity or listened to someone where every word is worryingly depressive of dismissive? Or had someone repeatedly standing far too close, you step away and they again step too near. They love your energy, but do you love theirs?

This is your intuition connecting.

I like to put on a cloak of protection as I arise in the morning and at any time during the day, I feel its calling. However, everything in life is about balance, so if you find yourself repeatedly putting on your energetic amour this can show a fear, so it would be good to look at why you have a need to be so guarded.

To apply your cloak of protection simply visualize yourself in a full length cloak, tucked securely under your feet, whilst giving out the intentions of protection and visualizing it in the colour of your choosing. I find Midnight blue a nice one to use, whilst pulling the hood up over your head to protect your Crown chakra. As I previously said try using this technique whenever you feel the need to safeguard yourself and your energy.

We can also carry different crystals to help keep our energy field in balance or for protection. Crystals I often choose for this would be black Tourmaline, Obsidian, Rose Quartz, Hematite or Smokey Quartz.

'Why would we even want to carry crystals around with us, some may think?'

So, from my previous writings I am sure you can see how valuable our energetic field is and when we start to understand a little of the way it functions, you can learn more about your inward feelings and even about yourself. The aura always works to enhance and protect. Everything is made up of energy including you, me, your favourite chair, your cosy bed, your fury friends etc., all created from how they have evolved, including everything they have been through and experienced, and also influences from the different elements being the sun, moon, wind, and rain with crystals coming from the oceans and Mother Earth. Everything in creation harnesses its own accumulated, specific energies, that's what makes us and crystals so individual.

When you hold or place a crystal over the body its energy interacts with your life force and can create either a vibration or feelings of heat or cold sometimes being felt, showing an imbalance in our energy field in the area this is experienced. As we have different senses such as seeing, hearing, smelling, or feeling our energy field can be constantly changing. Whereas the energy of the different crystals seems to hold constant. For example, a Rose Quartz crystal will always give out the energy of love, compassion, caring and can feel comfortable to carry or place on the heart chakra. Amethyst brings the energy of peace, calm, enhanced intuition and can be felt when placed on any area of the body, but is very beneficial around the head or the shoulders.

In the past the ancients viewed crystals as sacred and magical and not only used them for healing, but they also wore them for protection as well as adornment.

The native Americans used them in their ceremonies, embedded them in their breastplates and grinded them down to a powder to use in their face paints, as it was believed they would help protect them. To this day these traditions have been carried on and have stood the change of times. I am sure we all know that crystals have been created in the womb of Mother Earth over millions of years helped by the actions of the elements of the sun, water, wind and even volcanic fire and they carry the life force and energy from the earth and sky, with many stones having been used for thousands of years and new ones being birthed to help with modern illnesses and the pollution of the earth, sea and sky.

Thoughts

Certain years you will remember for ever – For me, 1987 was one of these: Meandering through shops searching for essentials which really weren't important but trying to create their significance, whilst also not seeing half the items displayed. Unconscious behaviour creating familiarity after unexpected shock and change that would last a lifetime. No going back to that ideal time where dreams were alive and life was a playground, with my beloved husband, two young daughters and my newly born son. In fact, looking at anything which caught my attention whilst trying to fill a massive hole in my life, time seemed irrelevant, and life definitely showed no meaning. How could life be so hard and damn right cruel, he was so young with no life's experiences. Taken at such a young age our baby son. (I share more of this experience and my spiritual learnings from this time later in my book)

A Child of Mine by Edgar Albert Guest

I will lend you, for a little time,
A child of mine, He said.
For you to love the while he lives,
And mourn for when he's dead.
It may be six or seven years,
Or twenty-two or three.
But will you, till I call him back,
Take care of him for Me?
He'll bring his charms to gladden you,
And should his stay be brief.
You'll have his lovely memories,
As solace for your grief.
I cannot promise he will stay,
Since all from earth return.
But there are lessons taught down there,
I want this child to learn.
I've looked the wide world over,

In search for teachers true.
And from the throngs that crowd life's lanes,
I have selected you.
Now will you give him all your love,
Nor think the labour vain.
Nor hate me when I come
To take him home again?
I fancied that I heard them say,
'Dear Lord, Thy will be done!'
For all the joys Thy child shall bring,
The risk of grief we'll run.
We'll shelter him with tenderness,
We'll love him while we may,
And for the happiness we've known,
Forever grateful stay.
But should the angels call for him,
Much sooner than we've planned.
We'll brave the bitter grief that comes,
And try to understand.

Messages

Shopping amongst strangers, with outward reactions, concealing deep emotions, or so I thought, until I felt an unexpected tap on my shoulder:

'I just had to share, as the sun from that window reflected, the most beautiful pale blue light radiated from you, but as soon as I turned to see further it was gone.'

How lovely was this confirmation from an obliviously intuitive lady viewing my aura? If ever you see blue in someone's aura, it usually insinuates healing. I will add that energy moves.

Have you ever felt a figure of someone standing very close, seen a dark shadow or a sparkly light from the corner of your eye, but on moving to view fully it simply disappeared, leaving thoughts as to whether you did actually see it? This is because it is energy and similar to water, as soon as there is a vibrational change in the surrounding area, such as the movement of your head or body it transmutes.

My guides taught me that our aura, or energetic body which includes our chakras, is pure energy which vibrates at different frequencies emitting varying levels of light, depending on how evolved our soul is and holds all spectrums of colour. It can change depending on what we are experiencing at the time emotionally, spiritually, or physically. Some colours are subtle and others far more dominant depending on our strengths, weaknesses and what is influencing our mind, body, and soul. Each colour illustrated in our aura carries a specific meaning and can be interpreted when understood.

Kirlian Photography is effective to help see the varying colours in your aura or intuitives can visualise to help one understand further.

Below is a brief description of some of the colours although they can appear in varying degrees from murky to bright which will obviously have an effect on the interpretation. If any colour is out of sync by being too faded, then healing and possible removal of blocks would help and if a colour is too excessive balance needs to be found in that area of their life as it will be dominating their persona.

Mauve or purple when visualised in an aura can illustrate psychic abilities, spiritual connections but also peace and calm. This person would benefit from meditation and spiritual development.

Blue, especially if a lighter variation, can show healing. Sometimes the person needs this or has strong healing abilities. It can indicate peace, calm and quietness but also relate to communication, especially if there is a shade of turquoise and visualised in the throat area. However, saying that, if blue was seen in another part of the body, communications, or expressions symbolic to that section would be significant such as the heart – maybe they need to communication from their heart space, usually with love. Dark cobalt blue can show higher spiritual connections and intuition.

Pink shows love, connections from the heart, kindness, gentle disposition, and compassion.

Yellow symbolises new learnings – especially life's lessons, spiritual development and wisdom, brightness and happiness in one's life or the area shown. Deep emotions can also be illustrated, but the colours of other areas would need to be taken into consideration.

Orange in the aura can indicate a time of facing one's fears, by stepping forward – not back, being courageous and becoming the person they really want to be. As well as passion, enthusiasm, sexual energy and creativity.

Red can indicate lots of energy, with a need to be grounded and productive. Red energy can be constructive which is passion and enthusiasm in anything you do or destructive which can lead to anger and frustration rearing its head. It can also reveal childhood issues influencing, especially when found in the base chakra area.

When **black** is seen, it often signals an unconscious reaction to pull one's aura in much closer to the physical body, usually for protection, inward reflection, peace, and solitude. Usually after a time of being strong for far too long or not being able to deal with life. Black isn't necessarily bad it can give a time of rest and recuperation but shouldn't be held for too long. When someone has a lot of black in their aura, energy healing helps bring light back into a dark field, which will aid the body to kickstart into healing itself with thoughts often becoming lighter. Depending on what part of the body seen, it can indicate a block or imbalance in that area. It can also illustrate a time of rebirth letting go of the past to allow the new to come in.

Grey or **silver** can be a very spiritual colour and a time of awakening. I have always been shown a very thin silver thread connecting us to the spirit world consciousness, which when severed is the time we return home. It can also show a temporary pause in life – just being, not making or wanting to change anything – content as it is for that moment in time until new inspirations appear.

Green can indicate personal growth, new beginnings, love, and compassion. We need a certain amount of green in our auric field to remain healthy and balanced.

Gold can reveal divine spiritual connections and understanding of life – enlightenment.

I mentioned previously that we have different layers to our aura, which include the etheric, emotional, and mental sections, (these link to the physical plane), astral (that is connected to the heart chakra) and the etheric template, celestial and ketheric layers (which are associated with the spiritual plane). I also mentioned you can learn from any emotions that have created a significant reaction from within, which at some level would reflect from your auric field and I would like to explain this further.

Trauma and inherited ancestral timeline reactions can cause blocked energy in these layers, which would at first have been felt in the emotional and mental areas of the physical body and aura. Because our feelings and thoughts create energy, a motion would then need to be initiated to shift it, such as talking, shouting, fighting, writing, drawing etc., These actions help transmute the vibration, which is good to disperse any obstruction in the energy flow.

This is sometimes the reason why, when someone really hurts, upsets, or aggravates you, it is good to express your feelings there and then. Obviously not in a negative way such as shouting and fighting, although at times this may well be needed.

Have you ever stood back, watched, and listened to a vivacious group of young men interacting especially if there are a few women with them? They will unconsciously play up to each other, whilst trying to gain superiority in the group, with instinctive actions putting any of the others down to attain their position. It's interesting how it will be aimed at anyone they find a threat or are too strong. Standing taller, expanding their chest area, or dominantly talking can be some of the traits. Most will respond accordingly to protect their own ranking, with there spontaneous actions instantly transmuting any excess energy build up within themselves, thus preventing weakness and fear. However, if one of them already has blocked emotions they have not dealt with, it may trigger an emotional reaction such as I have previously talked of. Their obstructed energy could trigger supressed reactions, such as stepping back and holding thoughts, feeling even responses within, until eventually the blocked energy builds to such a level, they will have no choice but to face what it has been showing them. This can often be a time in their life when they truly find their hidden strengths, although not everyone manages to do this and will carry on blindly.

However, on saying all this, life is about balance so being too strong can also indicate a defence built up to disguise weakness. Most strong people have felt weak or inferior at some point with bullies, narcissistic characteristics emerging as a protection to hide a weak disposition.

I love to include in my writings and teachings, relevant little snippets of information my animals have taught me over the years for you to also learn from and enjoy. We have all experienced or seen pictures of cock birds fighting, but did you know they can be kept quite happily together so long as there are no hens in the pen? The minute any are added, fighting for hierarchy within the flock begins. I find it so funny how it can be the same with men!

Also, totally irrelevant to anything I have been writing about, but gives a short respite and change of thinking from the previous readings. Something I was surprised to hear many years ago, so have never forgotten:

For an instance, just visualise how small and yes fluffy a newly hatched chick is. So, frail to the world, without food, water, and heat and when wet there is absolutely nothing to them apart from skin and bone. Did you know as long as they haven't had any food or water, they can survive up to three days? Obviously they would have eaten the yolk for nourishment whilst in the egg and this is a practice I would not recommend, but apparently used for transportation purposes in bygone days for day old chicks.

Sometimes when life has presented challenging times and emotions haven't been dealt with, there can be an unconscious reaction to try and blanket any feelings they emit. Some place them in a symbolic box, buried deep in the back of their mind, sealed very tightly and not allowing them any thought or heart space.

Most of you will recall turning away from something that has made you anxious or frightened, every time it was thought of or presented. However, there will always be a deep-seated fear attached, which if you turn and face would teach the biggest lesson on your soul's journey and end up being the best gift you have ever had. However, this can sometimes feel just too surmountable and another way to deal with the emotions attached to the fear is found, by releasing the compacted excess energy into something else. This will usually trigger compensating excessive actions, such as alcohol abuse, food (eating too much or not eating), overwork, play (too much or not enough), sex, compulsive shopping, etc., So, when the emotional trigger is evoked, it will be followed by extremities – feeding and masking the emotion, with a temporary feeling of fulfilment, followed by a downward spiral of guilt etc., coupled with the logical mind and heart reacting against each other and promises to change – until the next sensory bullet is fired.

So, when excessiveness is created through escapism tendencies from situations in their life they have felt out of control with, extreme indulgence can eventually attract in changes which often mirror the fear presented earlier, but in a different stance.

Life is about balance.
Drink to relax – not to escape.
Eat to survive – not live to eat.
Work to live – not live to work.
What possessions do I need to live the life I require?

Universal law teaches us balance. When something is removed, its place will be filled: when there has been drought the floods will come, when the leaves fall from the trees, they are replaced with new, when there is death, there will be re-birth and new beginnings etc.,

I saw a reflection of this in our flower nursery in various ways but will share just a couple:

Nature is a wonderful teacher of the laws of attraction. When there was an influx of wild rabbits, the foxes would appear. When they had eaten all the rabbits, they moved away to another food source area. When the crops of fields were waterlogged with heavy rain, the rats would be around until the crops grew plentiful again. Both laws of attraction with the animals looking for food sources and survival, but nature at its best.

Throughout my life's journey my guides often showed me how important self-expression was and how it could be implemented in many different ways from creative arts such as singing, writing, dancing, art, crafting etc., how many top of the chart songs have been written when the creator was going through one of the saddest times in their life and just started to write their feelings combined with music – which can give vibrational healing on its own.

Talking can also be an extremely effective form of release. Some, especially those whose throat chakra is fully open, will easily reply – sometimes with a dominant response and harsh expressions if the other person's words or actions have triggered a weakness inside them. Others joke or laugh to disperse a situation, but some will not express and hold within, which can start to cause a block as the situation will stay in their mind, playing over and over again which can throw their other energy centres out of balance such as the heart, solar plexus (emotional centre), even their third eye and activate a fear.

If you find it hard to express as some children do, it is good to write or draw whilst thinking about situations or people that have upset you. The actual action of writing or drawing will help to transmute the energy, but the most important thing is to then read any written words out load. These forms of expression help release blocked energy which is an excellent exercise to do when you don't have a therapist or trusted friend to talk with. Although this can be done at any time it would be good to do at the time of a full moon. The full moon is a brilliant time to highlight anything you need to release as it illuminates your pathway forward.

Make space for the new by letting go of anything you have outgrown and no longer serves you at this magical time of working with the earth's energy.

How To Do a Full Moon Release

Settle yourself comfortably into a favourite armchair or a tranquil part of your garden, at a time when you won't be disturbed. Play calming music or listen to natures song from the bird's tunes, the wind rustling fallen leaves, insects buzzing and even the sound of perfect silence, whilst allowing yourself to become completely calm.

I like to ground my energy first by holding various crystals such as Tigers Eye, Petrified Wood, Snowflake Obsidian or Black Tourmaline whilst visualising imaginary roots growing from the souls of my feet and penetrating into Mother Earth. I allow them to journey deep, far, and wide until they settle where they need to be, which is often in a bed of crystals or connecting with a stream running in the Earth's core.

I evoke the energy of my guides and Archangel Michael, who always comes with protection and his sword to help with cutting away my intended release, whilst asking for the highest vibrational energy possible, that is compatible with my own energy field to surround me at this time.

It is helpful to have pen and paper available to write down any thoughts or feelings. This can often be a time where we end up writing far more than ever intended with our guides assisting us to understand more of any painful times we have experienced. You may find yourself thinking of people or situations that have hurt you. Take a few moments and send forgiveness back to them. This doesn't mean that what they did was alright or acceptable, it just releases you from anything associated with them so you can move forward.

If you have previously written about painful events that you have not spoken about or find hard to communicate, this would be the time to read them out as load as possible, in order to help clear your Throat chakra. It is not for anyone else to hear, this is solely for you.

Afterwards burn them, rip them up or throw them into the sea. It is important to see them gone. If you find yourself not able to do this, why are you still holding on?

When we let go of something it creates a void, so it is important to fill this with something positive, fulfilling and especially heartfelt, so why not work on gratitude?

Spend a few moments giving out appreciation to anything in your life you have felt thankful for.

Thank your guides and Archangel Michael for their help, surround yourself in a pink cloak of protection and your release is complete. Remember the purpose of this release was to let go, so be careful you don't keep talking or thinking about the people or situation or its energy may return. Put your intentions into your new beginnings and especially what makes your heart sing.

Another way I often teach, which is important to do at the time a deep emotion has been felt is to express your feelings to the other person such as: "that made me feel ... so, can you explain why you said / did that?". Often the response will be far different than expected and not meant as it was received.

Our senses of hearing, seeing, feeling etc., reflect and attract what our vibrational energy is holding at that moment in time, from how we are feeling after experiences encountered. For instance, if two people were viewing a really beautiful, in full bloom garden, one could respond how lovely it was, whilst the other would only see all the hard work involved to keep it that way and not any of the beauty held within, especially if they were going through a hard time.

So, if our mind creates energy can you see just how important it is to keep a positive mindset?

'Remembering our thoughts create reactions which are our attractions.'

With no visual injuries, but pain more intense than being knifed in the heart. Outside reflections illustrating a perfect life, smiles, laughter excessive fun times, but when quietness falls the victim's mind begins to play, over and over and over again. No temporary pause or logical thinking.

How many times have you felt emotional pain, which just keeps playing out time and time again in your mind's eye?

If emotions aren't dealt with there and then, the energy from them can journey deeper and deeper into the auric field, until it hits the physical body and is expressed as pain or illness, giving no choice but to face what is presented. It can also be aches, pains, depression, tiredness etc., So you can see how my guide works with me with healing and understanding how our body's talk to us, if only we take the time to listen – healing of the mind, body, and soul. It is always important to get to the root cause of any disbalances. When we understand, we learn and grow enabling an energetic release, so important to protect general wellbeing and future life interactions from a balanced approach.

When someone comes to me for healing and we look deeper into the ailment they are experiencing, the feelings it is enhancing, coupled with the area of the body influencing, and my guides help, it usually takes us to an event in the client's life, they mentally and emotionally struggled to deal with. So many put big defences around painful experiences, attempt to walk away from, pretend they don't matter or try not to think about them. All evasive tactics, rather than facing what has been presented. When we are fearful and don't understand, we try to get rid of, destroy run away from. So many people do this with animals, insects, snakes, spiders etc., if they learnt about their instinctive behaviours, reproduction, and natural habitat, they could learn to understand and possibly respect them. It is the same with the emotional experiences, life presents us. Everything happens for a reason for us to learn and grow from, so make time for yourselves to journey deeper on mental, physical, and spiritual levels. Our experiences create our journey to enlightenment.

We all have free will and our communications can reflect our inner feelings at that time. So, if you find yourself moaning, complaining, running someone else down, recognise negative talking and simply change it to positive, as like attracts like. We all know the saying – my glass is half full or it is half empty, which one calls you? What you see in others is often a mirror of something about yourself you don't like or how you are viewing life.

When you arise in the morning try to start each day with a positive thought. These are words I like to send out into the universe:

'Divine spirit
Please can I ask for love and protection
for myself, my family, home, work, and animals and
gratefully receive any thoughts sent my way with love.
But please return also with love,
any thoughts aimed at me with ill intentions
Thank you.'

Every day is a blessing -
'An illuminated ray of golden sunlight cascaded
across the room,
as I lay listening to the bird's early dawn chorus.
Life so sweet, gifting me what I needed.
I am so grateful.'

Most mornings especially in the warmer months as we awake, I enjoy opening the patio door in our bedroom, allowing the cool, damp, morning air to fill the room, whilst listening to the early morning chorus of the birds and gazing out at the beautiful trees in our garden. Nature certainly lifts my spirit and sets me up on a positive note for the day.

'Don't worry, be happy
And then you will find
Life is so good with a positive mind.'

Just recapping on some aspects from the past few pages, in order to take you further with my guides teachings of the aura:

Energetic vibrations from your thoughts, feelings, health, awareness, and experiences are stored in different layers of the aura. The vibrations created can show through your actions, reactions, body posture, words etc., creating an oblivious mirror to the outside world, which attracts back your soul's requirements for future development.

'Sometimes, not getting what you desire,
can be a blessing in disguise as life unfolds.
The universe will always provide what you require,
not what you feel you need.'

Many people don't realise they can read auras. How many times have you looked at someone who is pertaining to be happy, but you just know they are sad? We have all experienced the magnetic feeling of a new friendship, when you can't wait to see each other again and soon find they are skilled in something you really want to do, have already faced what is affecting you, have the same interests or are experiencing something you have already gone through? People always come into your lives when that extra bit of help, support and assistance is needed to help you onto the next stage of your life, however it will always be a two-way link. Like attracts like with vibrational energy. Have you ever felt someone is standing too close, invading your space? so you take a step back, for them to move close once again? They like your energy, whilst theirs isn't compatible to yours. All of this is sensing auras. I love it when I teach my aura reading workshop as we look at seeing and sensing them, the representation of associated colours and how to alter your vibrational reflections to your outside world.

As I have already said it is very important to keep your energetic field balanced and a reason why so many people come for healing. Once they have worked with me initially, they then book in for what I call top ups any time they start to feel out of sorts.

When happy, relaxed and not under threat or ill your aura can extend anything up to several feet from the physical body with vibrant colours. Energetic vibrations from your thoughts, feelings, health, awareness, and experiences are stored in the different layers of the aura. Each layer moving away from the body increases in frequency, with the 7th layer having the highest spiritual vibration.

Chakras

Throughout our bodies we have many chakras, which are vibrating circular energy centres, that run through our aura and physical body from the front to the back, with each linking to a different layer of the aura. They draw vitality and light to us, but when obstructed they are unable to draw in the life force from the universe that keeps us balanced. When one is out of zinc it can also affect all the others. These blockages can happen from disharmony in our physical, emotional, mental, and spiritual situations. Healing helps free this, thus opening the chakras to receive universal energy.

Chakras can be seen intuitively, or their vibration felt, especially during healing, meditation, or yoga. It is very important after giving or receiving a healing session or any spiritual practice to close your chakras when finished, so you function from a grounded perspective.

Although we have many energy centres throughout our body, there are seven main chakras, which are the strongest. They are located on the body with the first one being found at the base of the spine and the last one on the crown of the head.

Crystals, colour, sound therapy and healing are good tools to use when trying to bring your chakras into ultimate balance. They have a natural healing frequency that resonates with the vibrational energy of each chakra. Crystals can be placed on the relevant chakras and healing can be asked for to balance the chakras in question. You can also work with coloured candles and meditation, whilst visualising the shade of a relevant candle filling the chakra and bringing it into balance.

These energy centres cannot often be seen with the naked eye but can be felt or dowsed over to feel their force.

The base chakra

This is found in the pubic area and connects to the first layer of the aura which is closest to the body. It is usually seen as red and programmed around the ages of 5 to 7. If it is out of balance, you may have feelings of insecurity, be ungrounded or have money problems. It is where anger and frustration are stored. When balanced you can draw on this energy to help you take-action, get things accomplished and survive. Crystals that I like to sometimes use on this chakra may be Garnet, Ruby, Red Tigers Eye or Bloodstone.

The Sacral chakra

It is found just below your tummy button, formed around the ages of 7 to 9 and is often seen as orange. If this chakra is out of sync, it may be visualised as a murky dull orange but with healing, certain crystals, or colour therapy it can be reactivated. It is linked to our desires, intimacy, joy, gut feelings, and intuition. I often find when this chakra shows up in healing it is a time for the client to face their fears, with change in their lives following. Energies from the emotional pains stored in this area can be transmitted to the first layer of the aura and physical pains can be experienced such as tension, upset stomach, headache etc.,

When balanced you can enjoy physical pleasure, good relationships, joy, creativity, and happiness. Crystals I like to use on this chakra are Carnelian, Tigers Eye, Amber, and Orange Calcite.

The Solar Plexus

Which is found in the centre of the stomach and is a place where emotions are held. It is often seen as yellow and is programmed around the ages of 9 to 12. When this chakra is out of balance you can feel very emotional, your confidence can be affected, as will your willpower, fears, and feelings of panic. These can all be accentuated, and you would need to be careful not to over analyse situations. Crystals I like to use when healing this chakra are Citrine, yellow Calcite, Sunstone, Tigers Eye and Rose Quartz.

The Heart Chakra

As you can imagine is in the chest area and is often visualised as pink or green. From here the chakras link into our spiritual side. It is formed around the ages of 12 and 16. When this chakra is out of balance, we can have trouble with love, especially self-love, often being quite unsympathetic or struggle in finding passion or enthusiasm in life. Crystals I like to use on this chakra are Rose Quartz, plain

Quartz, Amethyst, Malachite, Snowflake Obsidian, or pink Tourmaline.

The Throat Chakra

This is found in the area of the throat and is programmed around the age of 16 and is often seen as blue. This is our communication chakra and when out of balance we can have troubles with expression and experience irrational outbursts. Crystals I like to use when balancing this chakra are Blue Howlite, Turquoise, Blue Lace Agate, Lapis Lazuli, and Rose Quartz.

Third Eye Chakra

Found in the centre of the forehead and is often seen as a dark Amethyst colour. It is one of the chakras that help us connect intuitively and think logically. When out of balance we would find it hard to connect spiritually, have an unstable mind and could easily misjudge situations. The crystals I like to use on this chakra are Amethyst, Sodalite, Lapis Lazuli and Quartz.

The Crown Chakra

On the top of your head and visualised as white. White holds the spectrum of all the other colours and is the source of pure light and the spiritual source. This chakra is connected to our thoughts and when out of balance we will be unable to think clearly. It is through this energy centre that we are able to connect to higher guidance and spiritual wisdoms. The crystals I like to use when balancing this chakra are Lepidolite, Sugalite, Plain Quartz and Amethyst.

Higher Heart Chakra/ Thymus Chakra

This is one not everyone knows but is found between your heart and throat chakra and I usually see it as magenta in colour. It is the link between our physical and spiritual aspects. An area I encourage clients to tap when they are feeling stressed or anxious, whilst placing their other hand on their solar plexus, and taking three deep breaths, exhaling for longer than they inhale. This can help enhance peace and calm and to see things from a higher perspective.

We also have other chakras that have become more prevalent over the past few years, but I am sure those who connect with their guides and angels already interact with their vibration. These chakras can individually be intuited differently, however the basic concepts will be similar, so when you connect trust what your higher self and guides are showing.

The Earth Star chakra

Located approximately 12" below the soles of the feet and helps us ground and connect deeply to Mother Earth and her core essence. It is very important for this chakra to be activated when connecting to the higher realms. I always see this energy centre in earthly colours such as brown, green, burgundy, gold.

The Soul Star Chakra

Which is located in the etheric body approximately 6 inches above the Crown chakra and contains higher vibrational energy of earthly and spiritual knowledge. Where we can journey to link with cosmic wisdoms and connections to our spirit guides at our soul's level.

The Casual Chakra

Found 3 – 4 inches behind the centre of the back of the head. It is through this chakra we receive energy in the form of messages, information and inspirations with purity and love, from the higher spiritual realms to aid us on our chosen paths.

The Stella Gateway

Can be visualised approximately 18 inches above the crown chakra and often visually seen as gold. It is the gateway to higher connections such as the archangels, especially Metatron and pure energy.

Each of the 7 main chakras correspondence to 7 layers of the aura:

Etheric layer

This is the first layer closest to the physical body and the easiest to see with the naked eye. It relates to the general condition and health of the physical body.

Emotional layer

The second layer away from the physical body that links with our emotions and feelings and is constantly changing as a reflection of our present mood.

Mental layer

This is the third layer from the physical body and connects with our intellect, thoughts, state of mind, logic and ideas and belief systems.

Astral layer

Being the fourth layer away from the body it connects with our sense of well-being, balance in life, love, and our spiritual nature.

Etheric Template layer

This fifth layer connects your physical body to the spiritual plane through your sound vibration, communications, and creativity. I always say what happens on the earth plane is a carbon copy of the spiritual. As above, so below.

Celestial layer

This connects to our subconscious mind. A place where your physical and spiritual minds connect.

Ketheric layer

This layer protects and holds all the other layers of the aura together and contains the blueprint of our spiritual path containing your soul's experiences and events through time. Your link to the divine source.

It is very important to protect your energy field. How many times have you visited a friend, acquaintance or even someone who is ill in hospital and come away feeling absolutely tired and drained, whilst they look uplifted and feel great? Some will even say to you, I am so glad you came it has really boosted me, I feel very good. These are what we refer to as psychic vampires. Often, they don't realise what they are doing, but they like your energy and draw it into their vibrational field, whilst draining you at the same time. When I feel this happening, I will instantly close my core chakras, which are the main energy sources throughout the body, whilst putting on a visionary cloak of protection in a colour that feels right at the time, which I explained how to do earlier. In life there are many different ways of doing the same thing and it is no different when it comes to closing down your chakras. We can work through each one individually or simply give out the intentional request for all our chakras to be closed, a bit like a book being closed at the spine. They will all close down simultaneously. If it is really bad visualise a wall of the Hematite crystal between you and them. I find Hematite a great auric field protector and also grounder of energy.

I sometimes ask Archangel Michael in for protection. An energetic crystal shield of protection can also be created through visualisation. There are many ways of doing the same thing but as we are all different, some things will work better for you than others, so experiment to see which works best for you. Some of the crystals I like to use at times like this are:

Black Obsidian
This is a great protector of energies especially if it is a difficult situation. You can simply carry a tumble stone or wear a necklace or bracelet.

Black Tourmaline
One of my personal favourites. I use it a lot for grounding when I am working with crystal healing and grid work. I like to keep a piece by the main entrance into my home and therapy centre as it will stop those whose energetic field is not compatible to your own wanting to step in. I have gifted

pieces to friends and family to help with disturbed sleep because of dreams and nightmares.

Shungite

There are different grades of Shungite from the Elite to the rough water cleansing crystals which I like to use when making my flower and herbal essences.

I love to wear a piece of Shungite Elite around my neck or have on my table when working spiritually, especially when at fairs or events where there are lots of people.

Hematite

I sometimes use this little gem of a crystal when doing crystal healings on someone who has experienced a lot of pain in love to help create a Hematite protection shield around them as I have found it can help attract in the right vibration of love.

My dear gran's voice repeating her aged old sayings would often echo in my mind with this one being so relevant again now:

'Life can turn on a sixpence.'

But why did it have to be so true?

Turmoil and Trust

I couldn't concentrate on anything, my thoughts were all over the place, there was no way to ignore what had been presented, I had to make a choice between two pathways of which neither I wanted to take – what was life about?

Just as I thought everything was falling nicely into place, with everyday life becoming easier, exciting dreams of pursuing a career around my family and new learnings at night school, life delivered me a gift I didn't know how to accept, and did I really want to? How could I do it all again? I certainly didn't know and such a lifelong commitment. But to decline would go against every essence of my soul. On a higher spiritual level, I knew I would see this through, but my physical thoughts certainly had to catch up. This really couldn't be happening, especially at my age. It had never happened before, so why now?

With my husband at work, the children at school and my youngest son asleep upstairs, my thoughts drifted to the faint blue line on the test I was holding in front of me. No, absolutely no, this really couldn't be happening our family was already complete.

But why now just as life was beginning to get easier and dreams and inspirations becoming alive? Thought after thought, question after question, scenarios of what if all leading back to the same. Questions possibly never to be answered, but eventually an outcome which certainly turned out to be a blessing in disguise, once I faced the challenge presented and the beautiful journey with my youngest daughter. I now believe she was a special gift and has certainly enhanced our lives.

A friend is a friend to the end of the end, a lyric often used in song and also very true, so I thought.

A problem shared is a problem halved. When we go through something that creates emotional responses inside us it creates energy that needs to be released and as I have said before talking is a great way to do this.

Often a good friend is an excellent confident, however in my case this wasn't true and brought about the demise of what had been a beautiful friendship.

I decided to share my dilemma with a friend whilst asking her to keep it to herself at this stage as I hadn't made any decisions. This did trigger an appreciated release as expression helped ease the pent-up thoughts inside my head.

A two-week family holiday came in perfect timing. However, I was absolutely devastated to be congratulated by other mums on returning to the school playground. I was so pleased I had already made my decision.

Trust and loyalty are qualities I value in true friendship and once this has been broken, can be forgiven when the situation is viewed from a higher perspective and understand why a person acted in such a way because of their own personal journey, but our thoughts and reactions create energy which shifts and will not fit back exactly as before.

So, if a friendship suddenly starts to feel hard-work or you no longer enjoy their company, recognize the signs. How many times have you tried to keep doing something or seeing people you have outgrown, for there to be a sudden row or outburst and the friendship ends? This is the universe stepping in and bringing change when you have failed to make it yourself. We attract others to ourselves for the lessons our soul requires to learn. It is always a two-way thing. However, when everything we needed to learn from each other has been experienced the friendship will change.

> *'People and animals come into our lives for a*
> *REASON, a SEASON or a LIFETIME.'*

When new people or animals come into our lives it is often for a REASON, and to meet a need, we have expressed at some level.

They may have come to help you through a difficult time, to provide you with personal guidance and support, to aid you physically, emotionally or spiritually. However, neither of you are consciously aware of this.

Then, without any conscious wrongdoing, on anyone's part and often at an inconvenient time, this person will say or do something to bring the friendship to an end.

Occasionally they pass over, sometimes walk away or even play up and force you to take a stand. However, what we need to acknowledge is that our needs have been met, our desires have been fulfilled and our work together has been completed.

Everything in the universe is always a two-way thing. So, you would have been needed in their lives as much as they were in yours for the learnings attached to the friendship to be accomplished.

'Some people come into your life for a SEASON
Because your turn has come to share, grow, or learn.
They bring you an experience of peace, enjoyment, or
laughter.
They may teach you something you have never done.
They usually give you so much joy.
Believe it. It is real. But will only last for a SEASON.'

Lifetime relationships can teach you, lifetime lessons. Things, you must build upon in order to have a solid emotional foundation. Your job is to accept the lesson, love the person and put what you have learned to use in all other relationships and areas of your life.

'Everything happens for a reason,
both good and bad
and are the signposts through our life.'

'To the Mum I always loved, never liked, but learnt to forgive
Thank you for the lessons.'

Although I help so many people with their spiritual journeys and life's lessons, it does not mean I always see things clearly for myself. Whilst writing my book I was purposely omitting an emotionally hard part of my life that had been extremely painful to live through and was determined not to bring its energy into my writings. A technique or maybe a way of survival, I had learnt so well from my younger years of blocking out anything I didn't like or chose not to see. However, because of this I was not going with the natural flow and as these life's experiences contained so many different learnings that could help a lot of people, my guides had foreseen it very different to me.

They came through various students in my spiritual development circles, to convey an important message to me, that I needed to include a big part of my past, I had so far left out. When the message was repeated a few times by different people in other groups, I knew I had to take note. Our guides won't tell us what to do but will guide us especially if it is a big part of our soul's journey. However, it is still personal responsibility whether we choose to listen.

The next section of this book is very much about how I saw and felt my life to be. Obviously as children we can often see things very clearly, but sometimes events can appear much harder or bigger, than from an adult's perspective. My siblings and family may see it very different, but this is my own personal feelings of how I felt growing up, until my eyes were opened fully, and I truly started to understand.

I really didn't know how to write about it. As I have already said, I loved my mum, but never really liked her and the things she did. Although there were good times and I know she loved her family, she definitely hurt me very much. However, from a higher perspective, those we find most challenging are often our best teachers. Mum held out the behaviour and lessons for the best part of her life, until I finally went back to find out why and what it was all about. I had to be older, wiser and by then created a strong loving family of my own, before I was ready to deal with this. I had stepped away from mum and dad for a while, for this all to happen. Life had thrown me different experiences to work through out of the confinement of my birth right family, which helped me become much stronger and gave me the tools I needed.

I will say, at no time do I wish my mum any poison arrows. She was just a pawn in the game of life. If you remember me saying, we choose our parents for what we need to learn, mum also chose me, as parents do, for her lessons, which I am sure I provided.

As I was finding the writing of this part of my life so difficult, I surrendered it to the spirit world. The whole essence of my book is to teach others spiritual wisdoms from life's lessons, so if my guides felt it important to include my experiences with mum, then they really needed to help and show me how. Consequently, the next morning as I stepped from the bath, I had to grab a pen and a used envelope that was the only thing to hand, and the intuitive writing flowed. At the time, I really didn't know if it made sense, I just kept writing what came into my thoughts and later typed it up. I couldn't believe the deep explanations of what had been written. It helped me understand things and I couldn't have written it better myself.

As you read further, I hope you will feel the difference in the channelled spirit writings from my own.

All about Mum's inner struggle

– channelled through from my guides
Deep pain and hurt and the forming of a narcissistic
personality disorder.

'No-one will put me there again.
My own personal battle with the world not by my side.
The trigger,
Make me feel vulnerable, I will attack right where it hurts,
even if it takes weeks to plan.
Making you weak keeps me strong.
Giving you pain takes mine away.
Lost in a world of deep emotions,
Words locked in her closed heart not to be expressed.
Cuddles, kisses, any signs of affection indicated weakness
and vulnerability, upsetting the balance of the ugliness seen
in the world and self.
Emotions in her heart never to be released.

Oh, it hurts, it hurts so much what the eyes have seen from
a child's perspective.
But no-one, absolutely no-one will put me there again.
So, vulnerable, lost in a sea of deep emotions,
misunderstood, not trusted, or needed.
But I am not wrong, why can no-one understand me?
My children a part of me, will keep me strong
But again, nothing but betrayal as they leave their golden
nest.
I would have protected them if they'd stayed
I still love them, but they have walked away
Controlled love, manipulation, hurt – all followed.

by Lorraine Tricksey

My guides kept drawing my attention back to these spirit
writings, as obviously they needed exploring on a deeper
level. As I contemplated them, I was shown there were a lot of
teachings in each sentence, that needed to be expanded and
shared, so the wisdoms can help others explore their own
"inner journeys". I am sure you will all understand or relate
to them, at some level in your own lives. Either with the ways
you have reacted, or others around you have responded,
when a certain emotion was triggered, sometimes being well
out of character.

I was shown, some of these reactions are responsive
inbuilt defences, which have been built up over time.
We are all capable of putting them in place to protect our
own emotional self from further hurts. There is always a
negative, maybe hurtful, positive, or kind way through
anything – destructive or constructive. It is sometimes
good to remember, everything is personal responsibility

and if we start to feel our actions of self-defence are hurting those around us, then we need to look deeper and change our responses. We may have come through the hard times, understood the lessons shown, but in spite of everything continue to find ourselves responding in a detrimental way, which illustrates we haven't let go of the emotions attached and need to find a way. Possibly forgiving and re-opening our own heart for the cycle to be completed.

'I decided to forgive you
Not because you apologised or understood the pain
you caused,
But to gift my soul the peace it deserved and
yearned.
I never knew how strong I was
Until the time when I chose to forgive.
Someone who wasn't sorry and accept the apology I
was to never receive.'

Response

If we are responding negatively, we will attract that into our lives and possibly start to see everything around us in a disapproving manner. This in turn, will show in our auric field and influence how others see and react to us. I am sure at some point in your lives you have been associated with someone who has been very pessimistic and when your light is shining bright, it is very hard to be around them. You may notice this in their negative talking, responses, reactions or even the way they hold their posture.

When we are feeling downbeat, there can be a habitual feeling to revert to what I call the foetus position, a stance we unconsciously recall as safe. The shoulders can regularly feel heavy and ache, even pulled down and inwards. The whole physique can visually be seen to droop, almost into the stomach area, showing heavy emotions and the closing of the solar plexus, which is our emotional energy centre.

The auric field will also be pulled in quite close around the body, as when we are feeling negative this helps us feel safer. When someone is deeply depressed their aura will be dark. If not dealt with, it can affect the energies of the home, work environment and even animals in their lives.

It is never good to be negative, but there will be times when there is a need to withdraw. It is often in these silent moments, we find the peace and quiet required to enable us reflection time, to review the past and what has gone on around us and as we journey forward, will start to see our ways through. It can be a phase when it feels as though our guiding light has extinguished and are unable to see which way to go. Often a time of re-cooperation and rest follows before redirection starts to show. Sometimes, someone new comes into your life to point the way forward.

When feeling down or depressed, it is good to work with an energy healer, to help strengthen the body's energy field (aura), along with any medical practitioners they normally use. Healing can help bring light into a dark aura and lift one's vibration, often helping view life from a higher perspective.

Crystals

I have always been guided to work with crystals, using them extensively in my Reiki / crystal healing treatments and workshops. They adorn my own home and I usually carry some in my pockets. Each morning I self-select which ones I intuitively feel would be good for the day ahead. They will vary depending on what I am doing, where I am going, who I am seeing and also how I am feeling. The energies they emit can work almost like a magnet, helping balance my aura and energy field.

Sometimes, it is amazing how they come into your life when needed. You may suddenly come across a crystal shop you have passed many times but never seen, find some in a charity shop, have them gifted from a friend, or washed up on the beach shore. I have heard stories of crystals unexpectedly appearing in people's homes, with no explanation of how they came to be there.

When precious stones first find you, simply cleanse in spring, river, or fresh rainwater, to remove energies that are not your own and place them under the influence of a full moon to re-charge. If it is a few weeks away, then do it anyway under whatever moon cycle presents, as it is better than not doing them at all.

The full moon and a few days after when it is waning, is the best time for removing anything that no longer serves you, such as old habits, toxic relationships, negative energies, ending a business etc., At a full moon the earth's water table rises and can be very elevated. On a spiritual level, water is seen as emotion, and this is also a time when feelings can be running high. As the full moon begins to wane, water and emotions start to subside, so this is an excellent phase to work with omitting anything that is not for your higher good and a brilliant time to cleanse and charge crystals. It is an energy spring cleaning time, and you will see how much brighter the crystal's lights shine and how significantly more powerful their energies are.

Carry cleansed and charged crystals with you in a pocket, place on a bedside cabinet or next to your favourite lounge chair or an office table. There is no right or wrong place, the crystals energy will guide you, they just won't fit, feel, or look right in places they are not needed. Wherever they are put, their vigour will start to interact with your auric field and the energy within the room.

Smokey Quartz is excellent when dealing with negativity and blocks in life and can be very beneficial when placed in each corner of a room or house. Black Tourmaline, Shungite, Selenite, Rose and plain Quartz, Amethyst and Citrine are also others I like to use in my crystal healings when helping someone who is feeling down. Although as I work intuitively for each client, I will often select other crystals as we are all very different and complex, what works for one will often not work for another, but my guides always show me the correct ones to use.

Continuing with the further explanations of my channelled writings...

No-one will put me there again:

In a way, this can be a good thing. However, it is how you implement this into action going forward. Any experience we have previously attracted to ourselves which was painful, would have been put onto our pathway for us to encounter, learn and grow stronger from. If this event has taught us what we needed to know, we will have changed our persona, thought pattern and consequently our energy field (aura) and how we present ourselves to the outside world, which inadvertently would change what we attract into our future life.

For example, if someone had been bullied, this would only have happened as signs of weakness or feelings of being a victim were expressed through their guise, words, and actions. As a bully wouldn't pick on someone whose personality, confidence or image conveyed them as being twice their size and stronger or else the persecutor would probably turn out to be a victim. When we step up, become stronger, face any fears presented and truly discover what we needed to learn, then, **we won't allow anyone to put us there again**.

This doesn't mean to say you then become the bully and go around hurting anyone who releases the emotion of making you feel threatened or vulnerable. You work on yourself in whatever way is needed, possibly facing your bully, and stepping into any situations where you would normally have stepped back through fear and allowing yourself to be the victim. One of my favourite phases is, I am no longer a victim – I am a survivor. It changes your thought form from being weak to strong. Also, it is alright to say "no" when something doesn't feel right for you.

How many times have you agreed to do something you really didn't want to, as you felt you couldn't say no to the other person? When we are coming from a position of strength, we would deliver it with kindness, but it wouldn't be a problem to say "no". Sometimes by **not** doing the things we didn't want to, can force someone to take different actions or include another person, they wouldn't normally have asked. However, when the situation has evolved, the bigger picture can be seen and how everything worked out absolutely fine, often much better for everyone involved.

I am sure if you look back over your lives you will recall this having happened. The outcome would have been different but more satisfactory.

As we learn our lessons of life, our vibrational energy changes becoming lighter. As we let go of hardships, pain, negative emotions etc., and our soul develops further along its path, to travel back into these emotions and learnings again just wouldn't feel right.

My own personal battle with the world not by my side:

Most people have had times when they have felt completely alone – isolated, lost without a belief or sense, there is no one around they can trust or talk to, or have difficulty with others understanding their point of view or the true essence of how they are feeling. This can leave a sense of emptiness and isolation, where the darker times seem to get bleaker. It doesn't matter in which corner of their life they look or who they turn to, nothing seems to help or make them feel better, but the problem seems to get bigger and bigger, the more they think it over. In fact, everything associated with it, seems to be amplified enabling the feelings to grow stronger. Very much like a fear. Can you remember times when you have walked down a dark road or an alley? At first feeling as though everything will be fine, but the further you walk and the deeper you get into your journey, the negative thoughts and fears build, and you become convinced someone is following you with intentions of attack. You begin to walk faster and faster until at last, you find yourself running and your heart beats quicker and quicker, with your breath getting shorter and shorter. Until finally after you have built yourself up into quite a state, you find a safe place. Looking back, you wonder what it had been all about. Our minds can be so strong with the way we view things. Had a previous similar experience when the fear was justified been the subconscious trigger? This is the feeling of being alone with no-one there to support and help, when there is a deep inner battle going on inside your head. Your head and heart can also be in conflict. Common sense tells you everything is alright, but the mind keeps showing you different aspects of the same thing until you start to feel very alone and unsupported at that moment in time.

As I have said before everyone has their own personal journey in each lifetime, which will involve certain emotions with learnings attached to develop their soul's growth. We could have the same experiences as someone else but view and feel them totally differently. Our outside expressions can often be so different to what is going on within. We all go through challenging times in our lives and it is good to talk with others whom we trust such as friends or brothers and sisters, but when someone has been raised fighting with their siblings to get attention and does not have a strong parent bond, which may have stopped them forming close friendships, they can feel as though they have no one by their side to confide and talk things through and end up feeling as though they have their own personal battle with the world not by their side.

This is why I love to teach personal development and healing techniques, that can help us journey back through our timelines in order to heal the past, the present and consequently the future, with people becoming far more enlightened. If you find yourself beginning to feel out of sorts, start to make changes yourself. Go for a walk in the countryside or by the sea, nature can be a terrific healer. A change of scenery, doing something different, maybe meeting and talking with people you see along the way, this can all help lift your vibration, so you start to see the world from a different angle. Just don't keep doing the same things.

We are never left completely on our own. We all have spirit guides to help and guide us along our pathways. When doing palm readings, I often see a certain line on the hand, when this has been the case. It runs alongside the lifeline and is called a sister line. Often showing up when someone has gone through struggles and felt completely alone. It simply confirms the spirit world's support at this time in their life.

I am sure you all know the poem footsteps in the sand, which I would like to share with you:

Footsteps in the sand poem

One night I dreamed I was walking along the beach with
the Lord.
Many scenes from my life flashed across the sky.
In each scene, I noticed footprints in the sand.
Sometimes there were two sets of footprints,
other times there was only one.
This bothered me because I noticed that during the low
periods of my life, when I was suffering from anguish,
sorrow, or defeat, I could see only one set of footprints, so I
said to the Lord,
'You promised me Lord, that if I followed you, you would
walk with me always. But I have noticed that during the
most trying periods of my life there has only been one set of
footprints in the sand. Why, when I needed you most, have
you not been there for me?' The Lord replied,
'The years when you have seen only one set of footprints,
my child, is when I carried you.'

When this poem refers to Lord, I see it as whoever you deem to be your guiding light.

Our guides communicate with us in many different ways during our times of need, often making this connection in our dream-state. However sometimes, we simply can't recall them when we awake. This is fine, as the spirit world have been working with us on a subconscious level. If you remember the dream, take time to write it down and interpret its message. Pay attention to what it is trying to show you and act accordingly. Sometimes people have nightmares, but this can be the unconscious mind illuminating a fear we have and need to face, so it can appear as frightening. However, by translating the dream, we often see, it was trying to help, not hurt us.

When I was a child, I had a constant dream that continued into my adult life. It started with a tiny ball that grew and grew until it was so big it was about to squash me, but just as this was about to happen, I would always wake up. It doesn't sound very scary, but it always left me feeling horrible. One day when I was much older, I shared my dream with a spiritual friend, who simply said, when you have it next time, just change the ball into something like white light. Which I did and have never had that dream since. This visualisation always came when I was struggling with something or under stress.

How many times has someone spoken to you and the words expressed answered questions that had been going over in your mind? Or a song has unexpectedly played on the radio and the words have comforted your broken heart, reminded you of a loved one or guided future decisions. Have you witnessed a feather falling from the sky when no birds are around or found one in an unusual place? All can be reminders your loved ones, angels or guides are around and supporting you.

If a bird or animal draws your attention in the garden what is its message?

Have you ever asked for spiritual help and been shocked when it's happened?

This is very important, as so many people forget their guardian angels love to help. The spirit world will always support and guide us when asked but will not interfere. When you feel alone, stuck, or need help making decisions, require healing for yourself or someone else, simply ask for their assistance. It doesn't matter who you believe in, be it spirit guides, angels, fairies, God or loved ones, the important thing is to trust in the universe and send your request. Once you have evoked their services, let it go and don't keep thinking about it – just wait. Help will arrive in many shapes and forms and often in a different way than expected. Everything is always dealt with peace, love, and light, with the outcome being absolutely right for everyone involved when the full picture is seen. It may not be the result you wanted, but when everything unfolds you will understand why, and it will always be for every one's highest good. This is often the best thing to do when we just can't see our way through a situation – surrender it to the universe.

'The trigger – is it hurt, abandonment, abuse?'

With no explainable reason or pre-planned concept of time or events, the trigger had been fired. With breathing escalated until the heart felt as though it was coming through the chest wall. All thoughts irrational and misplaced, gritted teeth, clenched muscles, especially those of the heart, with the same constricted feelings inside the gut, calling to be released. Was it anger, fear or even sadness rearing its ugly head, which one sparked these deep-seated emotions?

An event, a reaction, followed by self-reasoning and justification that outcomes had been right – but they were not.

We have all been here, where something has initiated a deep-seated emotion and ignited a fire in your belly. You have reacted, often badly or unjust followed by your brain creating validation, your behaviour was needed or reasonable.

To start with recognise when this is happening and what has been the trigger. Why did you react? and acknowledge how you are feeling at this time and why? Is it the same trigger every time? maybe loss, a feeling of not being needed or something being taken from you, lack of control, misunderstood, disliked, or disrespected, non-acceptance or lack of love to name just a few.

It isn't bad to have a reaction like this, as now you can start to work on your emotions, understand the trigger and make changes. It may not be instant and could take a few times, but with practice results can be seen. Sometimes it is altering your mind set or talking yourselves into feeling a different way when the emotion starts to appear and take your first steps towards emotional freedom, a great technique to keep working on. It is important to make these changes when your reactions are beginning to hurt those around you. What may first start as an emotional outburst can turn into abuse, bullying, victimising etc., and many are unaware they are doing this. As you can see these destructive actions start from a point of weakness and can have devastating affects to those caught in the fire line, especially if it becomes a repeated pattern. Anyone who evokes these emotions are often a mirror for a deeper understanding of yourself, it would be good to view.

When someone has been hurt, abandoned, abused etc., they will respond accordingly and give out inadvertent messages to those around them, often taking on the role as a victim again. This is also why victims sometimes find it very hard to leave the person who has abused them. Often returning time and time again for the situation just to repeat itself. What is the abuser showing them? However, when they have been healed, they become stronger and change the vibration their auric field emits. This will change how others view them and attract the right people into their lives, with the old way of being no longer fitting.

'That which doesn't kill us only makes us stronger.'

'Make me feel vulnerable, I will attack right where
it hurts, even if it takes weeks to plan.'

On the following pages are further channelled writings from my guide, which help explain the words above. The first one is from my point of view and the second from my mum's perspective:

Me

I remember the happy times oh so well,
Sitting next to you with stories to tell,
The love of a mother, any attention was better than none.
The swapping of recipes, plant growing and fun.
But little did I know or comprehend,
the planned attack that would come at the end.
With defences put down, an open heart revealed,
The plan of attack would come into field.
By pulling me down and making me weak,
Kept you strong and me still meek.
I can't believe I fell for it every time.

Mum

But you triggered deep emotions of mine,
That I'd buried deep for such a long time.
I loved and controlled you unconditionally,
So why did you break free from me?
Now I'll play with your heart, I'll play with your mind,
Ruin relationships of any kind.
As you were born to be a part of me.
To keep me strong, why don't you see?
Your trophies were my rewards for doing so well.
I failed at school, now no-one will tell.
Because you are a part of me
You need to love me unconditionally.
I'll pull the love away,
I don't need to work – I'll sit down all day.
To scheme my next plan of attack to send your way
Now this makes me happy to see -
Not everything is perfect in your life, you've made without me.
You're looking too good today

So, I'll tell you your fat,

Which will stop all of that.

You've done well at school and in life which all can see

But none of this would have happened if it wasn't for me.

You need to remember where you came from.

No-one gave you permission to grow so strong.

So, don't ever feel you can move away from me.

Because you are a daughter of mine.

– by Lorraine Tricksey

'We are never given more than we can handle.'

I never understood any of the above teachings whilst growing up, mum's ways, her actions. I didn't need to, but I certainly felt the emotions.

So, what is Narcistic Personality Disorder?

As I understand it, the term narcissistic personality disorder comes from a myth about the Greek god Narcissus. He was the son of the river god called Cephissus, and a nymph Liriope. His whole persona was of arrogance, and he really thought a lot of himself and looked down on those who showed him love of any kind. Nemesis was a Greek goddess who served revenge, and always gave people what they deserved, especially payback when arrogance was shown to any of the gods. After noticing Narcissus's behavior, Nemesis led him to a stream where he could view his own reflection as he looked into the water. He instantly fell in love, without realizing it was his own image and the love could not be reciprocated. He died there, unable to abandon his own reflection.

Apparently Narcissistic personality disorder is one of a group of conditions, often giving the person unstable and intense emotions and a distorted self-image. They can put themselves on a pedestal and become obsessed with their self-importance and power. It often masks a lack of self-confidence, a deep sense of insecurity or lack of self-esteem. Many don't realise that narcissism can create a form of abuse.

A narcissist has no empathy and is attracted to those people they will get the most from. They will give them their pain to take it away from themselves, which makes them feel better when a certain emotion is triggered.

As I personally view it from the lessons learnt on my soul's pathway it is a horrible, and possibly a mental condition where the perpetrator views life from a very negative disposition. They have often been through terrible trauma at some point in their own life where they have felt very weak and wounded themselves.

However, they can also develop a heightened sense of ego where they can start to believe they are the best and put themselves on the highest pedestal, which no-one else can reach – altered ego. They choose their prey carefully and they will be the ones who can give them the most which can be love, financial, looking after possessions etc., which they will demand to fulfil their growing ego and to try and fill the emptiness in their hearts. I am the best, I need, you don't love me enough, unless … may often be some of the words expressed.

They do not show empathy, they are incapable of true love, but emotions can be easily expressed if it gets what the altered ego needs. Once they have chosen a partner their plan of action will come into play. Anyone who triggers them or has an emotional attachment to their chosen one will be got rid of in whatever way it takes. There victim will be unable to show love or affection to anyone else including a parent, siblings, and friends usually of the same sex as they will be considered competition to them, unless they absolutely adore the narcissist and play their games. Anyone who shows love to their victim is got rid of. Drama after drama will be played out. Lies, deceit all come into play until their plan has worked. Their victim will end up with no one around to emotionally support them. When the victim can no longer keep up with their constant demands with no-one around to love and support them, they will then turn on them, unless they meet their every demand, which will be very high as each demand is to try and fulfil the deep hurt emotions they inwardly feel, but it will never be enough. Hence why victims of this abuse will often never ever feel good enough. They will just keep trying until they wear themselves out, hence the saying will I ever be good enough.

In a normal family without a narcissist as one of the parents, mum and dad will work and rear the family together from a balanced perspective. When a narcissist comes out to play, they will be king or queen of that family and sitting on their throne will expect the other partner to meet their constant demands. Instead of rearing their children together and coming from a balanced perspective the children are often left to defend for themselves but should never disrespect the narcissist, even at a young age. They can often be programmed. Any that trigger them will be pushed away or punished. Any of the opposite sex will be used to keep the narcissist strong, they will have a use, and the one that is the softest or easiest to manipulate will be the 'golden child,' as they will look up and after them. Consequently, sibling rivalry can come into play.

Living with or leaving a narcissist is very, very difficult as they will make your life hell should you attempt to do it but then return. Often playing poor little me to win them back with lies and deceit always in play. Should you try to leave but return they will never forget that you have the capabilities of abandoning and disobeying them and will make life very difficult for you to break you down. So, in the end you will feel you can't ever leave, and all the problems have been because of you. Which leaves their victim very confused and always trying to rectify and please. They will be punished. At first often feeling as though everything is well and you have made the right decision to return, back to their nest. They will find your weakness and play on it. Until you feel too weak to leave again. They often have long memories and never forget so every time you trigger their deep-seated emotion their plan of attack will come into play.

If you choose to leave, keep running and never go back.

What is an Empath?

So, what is an empath and why do they attract the attention of a narcist, I found myself asking my guide one day?

Empaths can be very sensitive and highly in tune with other's emotions, sometimes absorbing their pain as they don't want anyone to feel as bad as they have at various times in their life.

I was intuitively shown a mirror image of a narcist and am empath, both echoing each other because at some point in their lives they had both been deeply broken emotionally. The damage occurred and since carried in the deep dark soul of the narcist reflects the deep emotional wounds held by the empath.

Consequently, the empath sets out on their journey to heal the narcist of their emotional hurts, without realizing their own subsequent actions are an effort to try and take their own pain away.

However, the narcist has no intentions of healing, only to inflict their pain and hurt onto those who draw near – if

I give you my pain, it takes mine away are the words I hear repeated in my ear.

So, you see here the law of attraction at play, drawing near what one's soul needs to experience in order to grow rather than what it wanted or would have chosen.

So, does an empath enable the narcist? I definitely think so, by the response I received from my guide in the form of a small verse:

'If you come to play with me
Guess what will show?
Pain, hurt, abuse and achievement
Of exposing your broken-down soul.'

*'When we hit the lowest point in our lives
Great changes can happen.'*

*'Concentrate on the opportunities of tomorrow
Rather than the problems of yesterday.'*

The result of living with this was my quietness, unable to express, nervousness. Being an empath with a growing narcissistic mum was hard. A disorder that overshadowed her soft, gentle soul. Emotionally I was always trying to please, rectify and do well, wanting to gain her approval, it never came, unless it enhanced herself. I found it so hard to trust. If you can't trust your mum, who can you?

When I look back over my life, I realise I have been guided and helped in so many ways, that has not come from my own consciousness. How on earth my siblings and I survived this as children I will never know, but it was not talked of by any one of us and certainly not understood. However, the teachings from it are what made me who I am today and have given me valuable tools to be able to help those who come to my spiritual practice for help and healing. I will never forget the stability from my dad, which will always be appreciated, especially when I was younger. He obviously had his own journey through all of this but why on earth did he stay?

'Mum, I tried, but you wouldn't let me help you.'

As I understand, when mum was young her dad had gone away to war. She always talked happily of these times with her mum and older sister, saying how well she was doing at school. However, she felt life changed, when she was around 6 years old, and her dad returned from war and subsequent siblings were born. She started to struggle at school and her older sister excelled in gaining dad's approval. I think she struggled to gain attention, plus as I understand it, he played one against the other. I can remember, when I was young, one of his favourite sayings was 'when my ship comes in, you can have' … as children you always believed in these dreams.

Mum's Consequent Reactions:

Innate hurt from her past, she had created a way to survive and protect her emotions. The after affects from war torn years and the return of her father into her life:

How can I be seen or heard? but it wasn't my fault.
Emotions not understood or expressed.
A once happy world shattered by the return of dad from
war.
A child lost.
No-one can really hear me, a child lost with parents
absorbed in their own realities.
Women second best – men's ego's,
I was strong and doing well before this.
Sibling rivalry just to be noticed.
Jealousy of younger siblings.
Lost in a sea of hurt and distraction.
Fighting with an older sister also craving attention.
Tried hard to gain approval that never came.

– Lorraine Tricksey

13th June 1984 was a day that would change mum's life for ever. Her mum – my gran, who we all adored, died from lung cancer. She had fought so well, and it was hard to see a once strong lady shrink to a fraction of her size, as the disease ripped through her body. She passed over at the young age of 63. So much changed in the dynamics of the family after this. Gran was the rock in all our lives and always managed to keep mum on an even keel.

This time definitely triggered emotions for mum. She had felt the loss of her own mum, once before all those years back, when grandad had returned into the fold, the subsequent siblings, with authority and discipline from a male figure all took its toll. I think she was at her happiest when she was very young, with her mum and older sister and was excelling at school. However, this all changed.

If you remember me saying, the same emotion will keep presenting to us until we learn the lessons attached. Mum struggled with her daughters marrying and leaving home, followed by gran passing over. All detachment of females in mum's life.

This can be a hard time for anyone as our children leave the nest. The house can feel quite empty. When my children started to leave home, my guide told me, that once they get to 18–21 years old, we need to let them follow their own journeys and shouldn't hold them back. We are there as a support and for advice, but they need to learn their own lessons, we cannot do it for them.

I was determined not to follow the same path as mum and when my daughters married, I viewed it as gaining sons, not losing daughters, and visa-versa for my own son. This is easier if you like their partners, but sometimes we don't and can see the flaws. However, it is not our choice. We all attract partners into our lives with the vibrational energy we are emitting and for our soul's learnings. Remember, when the lessons are served the relationship will often end or it could be a lifetime journey. We should never interfere.

Over the coming years, it became almost impossible for me to have a normal mother, daughter relationship and I came to understand why I had always been so protective over my siblings. It took me years to understand mum's disorder. I tried so hard to make it work, but each time it ended in mental or verbal attack of some kind. I ran away from it for a few years and started to create a family life of how I felt it should really be. I was determined my children wouldn't experience what I had. Each time, it was only the pulling to see dad that called me back. There would be no other reason to step foot back in that house.

Eventually, my guides kept telling me, I needed to learn the lessons attached. It was painful, but I had to understand why, in order for my soul to grow. If you remember me saying, we choose our parents for what we need to learn. What was it I had to learn? Because it wasn't going away until I had. At this time the blocked pain in my higher heart chakra, which is also our stress chakra, was so strong, I just couldn't clear it. I kept getting spirit messages from other mediums relating to my parents, and my friend Angela just wouldn't give up on the fact, I had to return. I learnt to step away for a few weeks, when mum attacked, but to always go back, at all times with psychic protection and surrounded in a pink bubble of love. I used my spiritual gifts to journey back into mum's timeline with her, which is how I learnt where a lot of her pain had come from.

I tried to help mum with healing which she would accept at times, but she wasn't ready to change, her defences were too strong and built up over so many years. Although I know at some level, she started to open her heart, especially when she managed to tell me she did love me. Was this genuine or because she was getting older and frightened of being alone? – manipulative love.

However, when mum wanted to join my spiritual groups, I had to draw a line. It was important to keep this part of my life and work separate. I never shared any of my knowledge about my guides and was really surprised when my native American guide showed himself in full ceremonial costume, to her during a healing session. She was so shocked she never forgot.

My mum also has a very strong spiritual gift, but due to her negativity and condition she could only see the bad in everyone.

A poem for mum

So, was it narcissistic personality disorder?
Or a way that was found to survive?
Pushing away the whole world
Rather than face the demons inside.
Who's in the mirror looking back at me?
Why do I not like what I see?
What are the wrong doings I have done in this life or a
past…?
That stops me wanting to see.
Why don't I deserve the good things in life?
I can't seem to let go of the control,
That boosts the need to keep hidden away my really low
self-moral.
The waves of disappointment keep coming
I just need to forgive the person looking back at me
Channelled through from my guides
– by Lorraine Tricksey

'Honour your teachers
Often those we find the hardest are our best
teachers.'

Nothing ventured nothing gained

It was the turn of the century, the millennium, and the year 2000. A very exciting time for my family. We had just moved, were living in two mobile caravans, and building our dream home. With the children still quite young, it felt scary watching the bulldozers demolish the old bungalow, knowing it was a point of no return. However, we had our visions and a journey ahead we were to grow so much from.

Have you ever had that feeling, the one when you walk into a place, and you just feel comfortable. When looking for a new home I believe a property chooses you. I personally know instinctively if it is right, the minute I walk through the door, this one was no exception. My guide has shown me how every house holds a different energy, which is what attracts you. When I was young, I remember the house opposite us really well. Different couples would move in, happy to be there and full of dreams, but within no time at all they were getting divorced. Later in life when I saw this happen again, my guides told me it was the energy held there, other places can be happy family homes. It's interesting how some of the old workhouses which have been nicely modernized, still carry the energy of hardships with money and the constant need to keep working to provide, which I believe, the type of families the houses call to live there need to experience. My guide has always shown me different houses attract us for what we need to learn.

It is always a good practice to spiritually cleanse the energies of a new home, using a candle and smudge stick. I open all the windows and doors and sweep the energies through the building, starting at the front door, as this is where most people enter and out the back.

Such an abundance of magical fae faces peering out from the Heartease Violas, delicately bordering the edges of my magical herb garden. With the striking bronze Fennel's feathery heads swaying in the gentle puffs of wind, teasing its leaves. Petite and intricately shaped purple-coloured, blooms from the Marjoram plant cascading down the aging Victorian chimney pot, meticulously placed under the extended boughs of the garden's healing tree, adorned with beautiful ribbons placed with intentions. Oh, and the delightful scents and varying colours from the Lavenders planted near the gateway, offering protection into this little part of paradise which always provides me with a step out of time.

This is the mystical and very special part of my garden where I enjoy growing different herbs, for my own use and work. I often grow them from seed and with healing intent and like to craft my own smudge sticks from them. Often under the sun, different moon cycles and solstices, depending on the intention of my work.

We have all visited places where we unexpectedly sensed fear, even though from our physical eye's view, there was no reason. It is just a vulnerable feeling of not being safe. It can also work the other way, a feeling of complete happiness or peace, which are good vibrations. This is sensing the energy of an area, which can change regularly. If there has been a row, illness, depression, hard times it can become stagnant or blocked. People visiting your homes will bring different vibrational energies, that may not be compatible with your own. So, it is necessary to smudge on a regular basis and is as important as physically cleaning. If you find yourself feeling tired, moaning, depressed or heavy, these are often the signs your home needs energy cleansing – smudging.

Afterwards everything often looks brighter, your mind feels clearer, and changes can be seen with plants and animals in the home.

To smudge you will need:
- smudge stick either handcrafted or brought
- candle
- Fireproof container
- bowl filled with sand

1. Find time when you will not be disturbed and can create a ceremonial sense of peace and intent. Call in your angels and guides and ask them to guide and help you energetically cleanse your home.
2. It is good to open all the windows and doors, to allow stagnant, blocked, or negative energies to leave
3. Light the candle and set your intention. I like to use a white candle for this purpose

4. Hold the tip of the smudge stick in the candle's flame until it lights

5. Move the smudge stick in circular movements, until the flame extinguishes and the smoke circles around, visualising that you are clearing away any vibrational energy that is no longer needed and for the energies of the home to be uplifted.

6. Hold the smudge stick over the fireproof container at all times to avoid any burnt cinders of herbs falling on the carpets etc.,

7. You can use a smudging feather to waft the smoke around the room, making sure it goes into the corners, as this is where stagnant energy can accumulate. If not just keep the smudge stick moving

8. Stay in each room for as long as you intuitively feel it is needed and the energy starts to feel uplifted

9. Always come back to the room and place you started.

When finished place your smudge stick in the dish with the sand and place in a safe area where nothing can be set alight. It will go out when all the negative energy has disbursed. We should never extinguish them. Always thank your guides, angels and even mother nature for the plant medicines provided and their help, it is always good to be appreciative.

If there is a lot of blocked energy, the smudge stick will really smoke, sometimes burning completely out. Do not allow your smudge stick to get damp or it will be hard to light. They should be stored somewhere dry, not where the air is damp such as a kitchen. You can reuse your smudge stick next time unless it has burnt completely out.

It is also a good idea to smudge your aura and anyone

else's who lives in the house including the animals. As we brush past each other our auras all intermingle and absorb the vibrational energies from ourselves and our homes. I often find when animals are brought to me for healing, someone in the home is also suffering from the same illness, emotions, or conditions because of this. Animals frequently show us what is actually happening in the home this way.

Always be careful when working with smudge if someone is asthmatic or pregnant.

Referring back to moving to a new home, it is always good practice to scrub the entrance steps, putting salt in the water, plant Lavender in the front garden or position a pot near the front door. Black Tourmaline is a crystal often used for protection and is frequently placed near the main entrance into any home. These are used for psychic/energy protection. Anyone who has a vibrational energy field compatible to the family living there will want to enter, however any person with ill intent or non-compatible energies, will not want to walk through the door. A bit like trying to make yourself feel comfortable in an area you know you shouldn't be in.

Different areas can be seen to protect themselves. Sometimes it is the wildlife that moves in such as bats, rare newts etc., nearly extinct plants and different trees, it's like a higher force coming in to protect that area.

I don't believe anything happens by coincidence. Everything happens for a reason at the right time.

I often find different areas present themselves to us, especially if you set an intention, ask to be shown and then wait until it calls you.

This was shown to me during a flower essence workshop, where I had been guided to work under the attractive, light green canopy of a beautiful Lime – (Linden) tree. A divine area that purely formed itself. A natural clearing was created by the neighbouring shrubs growing around and away from this spot, almost creating a circular effect. When I stood at the centre of this space the energies were amazing.

If a tree calls your attention, sit under its canopy, or simply place your arms around the trunk, as if giving a massive hug. Close your eyes and allow your feelings to flow, sensing the energies of the tree. Also visualise and feel its roots grounding your own vibrations. Every so often, it will send you healing and other times will draw healing from you. At the same time visually look at the tree, its condition, habitat, neighbouring plants, what animals visit and gradually you will start to understand why.

As I moved around the various trees which blended in the vicinity, I could feel their different vitalities. A stunning Eucalyptus, shredding its bark to reveal wonderful markings and overlooking the whole area, whilst intermingling with the Linden Tree, gave out quite a gentle feeling. This was surprising considering its height and size. The ornamental Red Oak felt very strong and upright, standing in its own glory. Whilst an Elm felt very vulnerable and took healing.

One day, I wanted to harvest some of the Red Oak's leaves for a class I was holding, to work with. I decided they would be absolutely perfect for the teachings, with their distinct shape and markings of the well-known oak leaves, but much larger in size, so easier to use. One thing I teach when working with Mother Nature is to show respect and to always ask the plant or tree for permission before taking. There was hardly any wind, and the branches were quite still, as I stood in front setting my intentions and waiting for an answer, which came pretty soon. The branches nearest to me and in my height, range started to lift away. I stood and watched, and this action was repeated, it was telling me no. I moved to another area of the same tree and tried again, only to get the same response, so I left the harvesting of these leaves alone. For some unknown reason, it wasn't to be that day. Plants or trees which are ready to gift, will lower their bows to you, sometimes quite considerably.

It doesn't matter how much we desire a plant, and our needs could be very high, we should never take if permission isn't given. Another plant will be presented to us, when the time is right and if we connect, craft, grow or use the plant in the way shown, we will begin to understand why. It usually turns out to be a better choice, with Mother Nature teaching us what we needed to learn. The plants survival needs to outweigh our own requirements.

When gathering plants, only take what is needed. If one is very tiny, set your needs aside and don't harvest. Try and help the plant in some way to grow and spread. Harvesting can come at a later date and there will be more to share with others. If help is needed such as watering, feeding, de-heading or removal of dead wood, it is good to help. As we give, we receive, often in ways we wouldn't expect. However, never give in the hope of receiving, if our intentions are wrong it will work differently.

Plants will often self-seed in certain areas if they are needed there for the people, animals, or environment. If one suddenly starts to grow in your garden look further at what it is showing you. I find it amazing how many wild herbs start to grow in old car parks or disused factory units. They often come in for their energies to cleanse and heal the locality.

Referring back to areas choosing you, during one of my flower essence workshops, everything had been set to work under the Lime tree and whilst it all went to plan whilst crafting the tree essences, when we started to connect and craft with Selfheal for a flower essence, we were guided to a lawn area. At first, we didn't understand why, it was purely intuitive and a feeling of being blocked as we walked towards the Lime area and a free flow of energy, when guided towards the lawn.

When you become more in tune with energies, you can feel obstructed, heavy, or even stopped when entering certain areas, if they are not right for you at that time.

Selfheal is an ancient herb and has a long history of medicinal use and being applied to wounds to help them heal. Nicholas Culpeper a 17th century botanist, states it is called Selfheal as 'when you hurt, you may heal yourself'.

So why was the lawn area calling us?

On reflection, everyone had been drawn to stand in different areas on the grass and had instinctively positioned their essence dishes on the lawn in front of them. They all contained natural spring water, infused by the sun during the Summer Solstice and the ancient herb – Selfheal. At some point, it was noted that the spot we had been intuitively called to, had Selfheal growing amongst the grass. It had been difficult to see at first, as it had not yet flowered. Nevertheless, it was very interesting to realise how much nature can guide and help us. We were working with Selfheal and had been taken to a space it had chosen to grow naturally.

When working with flower essences it enhances them when placed amongst the flowers or herbs as the water will absorb and hold the plants vibrational energy.

The positioning of the bowls created a distinct shape. So, what was this directional arrow showing us?

It was pointing energy away from a property I had been called to work on a few times before. You may remember me explaining about the energies certain houses hold, this one was no exception. Its last owners had just moved out to a nearby town. Visually it was an exceptionally beautiful property. This house was haunted, and the owner had a brilliant photo of a spirit lady who resided there, showing herself in her bedroom mirror. The spirit lady loved the house and certainly made her presence known. I saw her walking the hallway with white sheets and lavender, which in past times would have been stored between the sheets to keep the insects away. She had previously come through showing how sad she was, as there were no longer cottage flowers in the garden, it wasn't loved as she had treasured it. Whilst still living there, the owner who had since moved, wanted to connect with her spirit, so when she sensed her around, sat quietly and communicated with her via her mind and thoughts. Telling the spirit lady how much she also loved the property and wanted to make it a home. She didn't want to cause any harm but wanted to bring back its attractiveness and character once again. In effect, she wanted to work with her, not against her.

The present owner started to feel inclined to fill the gardens with cottage perennials, roses, and ancient herbs that she was called to and also loved.

Eventually the gardens were once again full of flowers and colour, which attracted back the wildlife – the birds, bees and butterflies and brought the owner and spirit lady great happiness and healing. So as this lady moved out her work there had also been done. Were we being called for the next part of that areas self-healing, by removing any residual blocked energy as the new people moved in?

It's interesting to note, this was a very old-thatched cottage which was over 400 years old and steeped with history – smugglers, linked to the Duke of Monmouth, workhouses all of these times added to the different energies in the home. So, whilst the last owner had connected with the spirit lady of the house, there were so many other layers that also needed connecting with and possibly healing.

Not all were bad, but there had been a lot going on for centuries and certain hardships had definitely been experienced there, leaving their residue in the energy of the home. This would have been felt at some level by the people drawn to the land and home's vibration, but also for them to learn from or else it wouldn't have called them.

I had a lady come for healing, in the same time frame, I had been working on the energies of this home. She didn't reside in the area anymore but had lived in that house as a child. So once again you can see synchronicity at work. She was recommended to come and see me for healing by a friend who knew nothing of her living there in the past. In fact, as we walked to my healing room, I recall her saying I am sure I used to live near here when I was a child and when she mentioned the name of the house, I was able to confirm which one it was, the same dwelling whose history had been showing itself to me.

Healing often takes the person back to the root cause of a problem. Most of the emotions attached to this had started whilst my client lived in this home as a child.

Some months previous during one of my meditation/

development circles, spirit had shown us a large barn fire connected to this area. It was frustrating as I didn't know the history regarding this at that time, so confirmation couldn't be given. However, I always trust what we are shown and at this time asked my guide to give me more proof or lead me to where I can find out more information. It was amazing, just these few months later, whilst talking with this client, she recalled how a fire had happened whilst she was living there, so confirmation and details were provided.

I decided to work on this further during my circle, however whilst we were all meditating, there was such an almighty bump and I mean an almighty bang, almost like someone had thrown a sledgehammer on the roof of the building with all their might. I decided someone wanted it to be left alone.

One of our houses we purchased to demolish and follow a dream to build our own home, had previously belonged to a retired doctor who had passed over. Whilst trying to buy it, we had submitted our offer only to have different builders try to gazump us, going quite a few thousand pounds higher. My guides kept showing me things would be fine, but it was a very stressful time, as most house moves are, so it was quite hard to trust. However, they weren't wrong, and the sellers stuck with our offer. It had a lovely-homely feel, and I always felt it wanted to remain a family home and not over developed.

It took us the best part of two years to build our new home, whilst living in a couple of mobile caravans on the site. It was hard work with our 6 children still young, doing as much as we could ourselves on the self-build, as well as working and finding extra money to fund it. But we always reflect back with fond memories because it was a dream come true.

I will never forget our pulling down party, held the weekend before the bulldozers came in, with our family, neighbours, and friends. It was a shame we couldn't have kept some of the writings on the walls.

During these couple of years, it was fun having barbecues outside, as it was easier than trying to cook inside the caravan and doing a juggling act with the dinner plates on the limited worktop area. Bathing in the tiny shower cubicle was an art in itself, but at least it always had a good supply of hot water. We soon learnt to keep the wardrobe doors open, so as condensation and the dropping temperatures didn't cause mildew on our clothes. The number of times I would run bare foot over to the outside shed which housed the washing machine in the dark, as we had been busy all day and forgotten to wash the school clothes for the morning. Plus, the summertime scorching hot days when the heat inside the caravans felt as if it were some 100 degrees. All silly things which we take for granted when life is normal.

Apart from the little annoyances living in the caravans was fun. The children played and ran free outside and helped us when they could. Winter night times, when the dark nights ceased work and play, were cosy, sitting around the gas fire watching telly, reading, and playing games. There was always something to do. Our lane down the side of our property led us into the forest behind, which was a great place for long walks, bike rides and taking the dog to swim in the river.

I don't think any of us will forget the cold winters when you could see the frost on your breath as you huddled under the bedclothes to keep warm. I always had the job of a Mum, getting up first to turn on the gas fires, so there was some warmth for everyone to get dressed before school. Not to mention the winds that ripped around the outside of the caravan and watching the swaying of the trees not too far away, praying a limb wouldn't break loose.

It was great seeing our new home take shape, from the footings up to the roof, which we designed with different tile details and finials. Being so pleased and feeling we were nearly there when the roof finally went on, to only realise this was about a third of the way through.

We worked hard over these couple of years, not only with planning how we wanted everything to be and the building work, but also sourcing the supplies we needed at affordable prices, which had to happen for us to complete this project. At times, we sourced supplies at such a good price we would buy a few, keep what we needed and sell the rest, which then paid for the ones we had used.

Any new ventures usually bring some degree of stress, hardship, hard work and commitment. However, those things we have to truly work for are often our best achievements that we learn and grow from, and we were extremely pleased with the end result. Even though we have now moved Grey Willows will always be a part of us, as we followed our dreams, and our hearts were captured.

My guides were around me at this time, I always knew they were there. However, when we have something major going on in our lives such as this, births, marriage, divorce etc., they will step back to allow any lessons to be learnt. You may feel a distance as your minds are elsewhere, but if you can take the time to sit quietly and connect you will realise that they never leave you and are actually supporting you through the hard times.

Once the house was finished my guides started to show me, I needed a separate workroom away from the home, to be used solely for my spiritual work, which was ready to be taken onto another level and for the right energies to be able to build. This happens when we spiritually connect, cleanse, and protect the vibration in the same area over a period of time. It helps make spirit communications with us much easier. I also started to realise that as soon as clients entered my therapy room the healing commenced. Without initiation, they would unload problems, talk of their aching or ill bodies, recall childhood experiences, becoming more uplifted and even look different than when they first arrived.

If we allow anyone or even temporarily store different items not connected spiritually into our sacred space, it can interfere with the divine energy flow. The vibrations need to be nurtured, balanced, and protected – basically creating a sanctified area to work within.

The children were getting older, family life was busy and hectic, and I loved every minute of it. However, my guide kept showing me, the lively energies of the home, didn't blend well for my spiritual work, even though the children were usually at school or asleep, their vigorous vibrational energy could still be felt and disturbed the essence of a spiritual sanctuary.

The ideal area for my workroom soon presented itself, overlooking the garden. It was a quiet, elevated spot, under the shade of some beautiful pine trees, that suddenly started to call. It was the perfect place for a summer house, for my spiritual work. Matt, my husband, created a beautiful space for me. He has always loved and been very good at crafting, repairing, and building.

It was a bright little chalet, nestled amongst the trees with a few steps leading up to it and a little veranda where I hung wind chimes and wild bird feeders, I thoroughly enjoyed working from here. It gave me peace and quiet away from the hustle and bustle of the main house, with its serene energy, in the middle of nature. Far better for my family and my work was able to grow. I continued with my readings, healings and started holding meditation / spiritual development circles, teaching Reiki and crystal healing – beginners and advanced workshops, animal healing and communication days, tarot and palm reading courses and held psychic fairs at local halls to help the people I taught, get started.

Do you believe in coincidences?

Have you ever thought of someone only to find them knocking at your front door or telephoning a few hours later? and isn't it amazing, how the right people seem to come into your life just at a suitable time?

It could be someone who has already experienced a difficult phase and come to help you through something similar, such as a death, birth, divorce, redundancy, illness etc., My spirit guides and the universe never cease to amaze me with the way they bring situations and even people together at just the right times.

Whilst working in my spiritual retreat, a client came for healing each week, who was a driver for a local car parts company and knew my husband through his work. Although, I always keep client's details absolutely confidential, she specifically requested I didn't let my husband know she was seeing me for healing. However, I did point out that he was often around, so it may be difficult not to bump into him, but I definitely wouldn't be sharing anything about her treatments.

Do you remember me saying how our actions create reactions and our auric field reflects the energy from them to the outside world. Consequently, if we do things for the wrong reasons such as stealing, gossiping, lying you may feel no one will ever know, but it will show in your vibrational energy and the way others perceive you. So, in the long run you will also be ripping yourself off.

Have you ever met someone and instantly distrusted them even though you had no reason?

The lady came for a course of treatments over 6 weeks and not once during this time, did she meet my husband, until the last session just as she was leaving. I smiled to myself as I heard her telling him how surprised she was, they had not met there before. The spirit world will always help, I believe sometimes even block things from happening if it is our request or not for anyone's higher good.

It was a beautiful August evening, you know the ones where the sun has gone down, dark has descended but the air is still warm from the day. Remnants from the home cooked buffet and empty drink glasses covered the tables as a wonderful night celebrating a friend's birthday with a small group of like-minded friends drew to an end.

Such a lovely gathering held in her garden, which was not particularly large. A group of about 25 people, so why hadn't we seen one of my relative's ex-wives? Apparently, she was there all evening, also enjoying the party. To this day, I don't know how my husband, or I never saw her there, we thought we had mixed with everyone. Quite a few years had gone by since we had last met, as she had moved to another town some distance away. So why had my friend come into her life, and we had all been at the party together, but not met? There were definitely higher forces at play that night.

A few months later with my same friend, we initiated some people into their Reiki Master's Degree with one of the students being this lady's mum and that was the last time I saw either of them.

Sometimes, we don't know why people come back into our lives, but there will always be a reason, possibly a lesson or emotion to be released.

I believe when we work spiritually, it is also good to have something from the physical plane or everyday life we also enjoy, as it helps keep us balanced and grounded.

Animals have always been a big part of my life and whilst living at Grey Willows, the house we built, alongside my spiritual work, I continued hatching our chicken, duck, and geese eggs. This grew into a small business and become a very special part of our lives later on.

A local elderly lady used to call occasionally for eggs and also purchased chicks and ducklings. We would chat and she loved to watch the progress of the house. We had 9 happy years living there and when we eventually put the house on the market, she ended up buying it. I always smile to myself when I recall this memory, as her husband never set foot inside, until the day they moved in. He had left the whole move totally in her hands.

At the time we moved into Horton Vale Nursery, which we later formed into The Healing Garden Centre, the animals were a big part of this venture, along with my Spiritual Learning Centre and the herbaceous plants. It took a few weeks to get settled and ready for business.

I was shocked when we decided to open the nursery to the public early and our first customer was Heather, the local elderly lady. She had coincidentally decided to pay us a visit that morning just in case we had summer bedding for sale. It was nice to have a friendly face as our first customer.

> *'Was it a dream, or experiences from our lives'*
> *timelines that created the inspiration to build our*
> *own home?'*

The colour was fading from his tired eyes, showing me life beginning to withdraw. The past 80 years had taken their toll on his now tiny, pain ridden body. The enthusiasm and love for his beloved canaries waning, being replaced with negative speaking.

But I loved seeing a spark of life, as we recalled memories from my dad's past to help me with my book, regarding my roots, timeline, and traits. I had un-subconsciously carried so much forward, just by following my own heart and what felt right for me and my family at the time – spiritual gifts and wisdom, animals, creativity in crafting and plants, building and business aspects. It was the energy I had been brought up in, that influenced my future, even though some of it happened before I was born. Showing how our past timelines, carried through from our ancestors to ourselves, can influence our future.

As I relay memories from my father, you will begin to understand why his dad, my grandad's spirit connected in with me, whilst I was setting up and running the Healing Garden Centre.

My dad, his brothers and my grandad were all builders

by trade. I found it interesting to learn that this grandad did the brickwork for the Sandbanks Hotel in Poole, Dorset.

I would just like to remind you of the effects of the war and the hard times it brought for families to survive. However, these were events and experiences that made them who they were. All hardworking men, who didn't just sit back and have everything handed to them on a plate. They had to go out and find work, food, and money for their families. By using what they had and learnt along the way. It created a family life that has passed down generations.

My guides have often said to me, when life has been hard, try harder. It will bring in new directions, you wouldn't have explored, if these times hadn't shown. A practice I have always followed and has never seen me wrong and one I teach my children today.

When life is difficult, dance with it – "sink or swim". It is trying to help, not hurt you. When we are going along our pathways and the journey starts to get steep, it is often life trying to pull you in a different direction. However, we can be creatures of habit and like what we know, the unknown future can appear scary. Life can sometimes be like wearing an old, worn-out pair of slippers. We continue through it, just putting up with things, no matter how bad or uncomfortable they get.

There is a well-known saying:

> *'If you keep doing what you are doing,*
> *then you will keep getting what you are getting.'*

Nothing will change and lessons being shown, will not be learnt. However, if we choose not to make changes and they are needed for our soul's progression, often the universe will step in and make them for us. Sometimes, it can be harder than if we had made them ourselves.

For example, staying in a job you are not enjoying, just because the money is good, or it provides a stable lifestyle. When the universe steps in, the job will be lost, and the person may then pursue a hobby as an income. As they are then doing something that makes their heart sing, success will often follow or a better way of living. On reflection and having come through the changes, they will be pleased the redundancy happened.

'Success grows where energy flows.'

Once, I had a couple of clients, who didn't know each other at the time, coming to my circles. Each week, I would hear them saying how unhappy they were at work. However, I remember them both being mortified when at different times they were served redundancy notices. Their jobs were never going to work, as they both hated being there and didn't have any passion for what they were doing. One of them was also beginning to experience ill health, which got so much better after she left.

When we are bored with life or not doing what makes us happy, we can often feel really, really tired. In fact, so tired we can start to feel ill. When we have a passion for something, our mind and energetic body lifts, as does our energy levels and this tiredness often goes. Our thoughts create our realities which can affect our lives. So, it is important to keep passion for life alive be it work, hobbies, new learnings, different interests etc., Try and go somewhere you have never been or do something you haven't done before, as often as you can, to gain new experiences, meet different people and keep a zest for life.

As the people I have just mentioned didn't make changes themselves, the universe stepped in and did it for them. They both went through a time of having to trust another job would come. It was interesting to see how they both survived over this drought period, however, we are always looked after, even if we can't see it at the time. One was given a redundancy package which helped her with the next stage of her life and the other had different small jobs come in, which when added together helped her survive this time, different skills were learnt and eventually new employment. They both also had a fear of not having enough money, which had been passed through from their childhoods when money had been scarce. However, by trusting the process and the spiritual guidance they received whilst coming to my groups, they began to see the bigger picture which also helped them override this worry. When we face our fears, we become strong, when we let them encompass us, we remain weak.

My guide used to say to me, when you can't wait to go somewhere, be it work or a hobby, you are doing the right thing. However, if you find yourself being constantly late, missing days or even dragging yourself there, these are signs you have outgrown what you are doing, and change is needed.

I always pass this on to students who come to my spiritual circles. When you can't wait to get to them or keep thinking about it in the week, then the circle is still for you. However, when you start to miss groups or no longer have that excited feeling about coming, then you have outgrown the circle and it is time for you to leave. The teachings have been completed.

My guides encourage me to learn different skills, especially with my spiritual work, bringing different teachers, together with life's lessons onto my pathway when the time is right. They tell me we should never stop learning – life holds many wisdoms if we take the time to see.

'When the student is ready the teacher will appear.'

I often teach my students to have their fingers in more than one pie, when it comes to work, especially if self-employed. When one part goes quiet, as it can so often do, especially with different seasons, you always have the other skills to fall back on. It also keeps interest, as doing the same thing day in and day out can get a little mundane, and some parts of your work can complement others.

Referring back to the influence of my roots, timeline and the building of our own home, my mum's dad, my other grandad, was also a builder with his own construction company and built whole roads of houses, such as the ones he built in Redhill, Bournemouth. He even named one after my mum and sister, called Deneve Close, and the bungalows in the older side of Colehill, Wimborne, Dorset, finishing up building in Bridport. His sons, my uncles still run the business today.

My paternal grandad was a very good businessman, who learnt as he grew but started with nothing and worked his way up so, you see building and construction were on both sides of my family. With the construction work, there was always clearing of sites and tidying, which helped create perfect bonfires and memories I will cherish forever.

It was a dark winter's night. The air was crisp and damp and each breath I took tingled my nose and encouraged laughter, as long hauls of mist left my mouth. The sky was clear, as frost was pending, and the stars sparkled like little power packs of magic, torches from our loved ones. There was an air of excitement, as the night was bonfire night, which I would get to spend with my family, grandparents, aunties, uncles and all my cousins. We would gather around a massive bonfire, which had been compiled over weeks, from my grandad's construction business and the Autumn trimmings of their garden and hedgerows. This was a yearly event we all looked forward to.

The smell of roasted chestnuts, baked jacket potatoes, hotdogs and fried onions cooking filled the air. Handmade, sticky, toffee apples, which always got stuck in my hair, were passed around. Our tongues were burnt from the toasted marshmallows, but it was all so much fun. We lit sparklers and ran around spelling our names and the air was filled with our constant giggles as we ran free. It was always finished off with the display of fireworks our parents had all contributed to.

Somehow silence would fall, as worn out we would huddle around the fire watching it dance and crackle, its ambers burning bright and the remnants of another lovely evening making beautiful memories. Through the smoke from the fire, I could see the contented face of my gran, so proud to have all her family around her.

So why, after such a beautiful evening and for some unknown reason, would everything always change? A row would erupt with mum in the centre, and we would leave with her in floods of tears, emotions not understood and fighting with brothers and sisters to gain attention.

Although, both grandads had passed over, by the time we built Grey Willows, they had all been great teachers, helping create an environment around me and influencing in some way, the life I was to lead. Like I have already said, we choose our families for what we need to learn in this lifetime.

'Sometimes in the winds of change we find out true directions.'

How Horton Vale Nursery found us

It was a sad time in our lives, as my lovely mother-in-law was terminally ill with cancer, some of our children had flown the nest and our self-build home was beginning to feel too big for just the few of us. However, my guides were showing me, my spiritual work was to go onto another level.

Times were changing and there was restlessness in the air.

On hearing the click of the letterbox and our dog, Benjie's ceremonial barking session, I went to investigate. My eyes were drawn to the local Advertiser paper, by the front door. Being in a pensive mood, I quickly flicked through its pages, looking only at the main articles, when I saw a house with a flower nursery attached, advertised for sale. I remember thinking, if I was to move, I would love that one, but with so much going on, it isn't going to happen. Then I promptly put the paper away. I was shocked when later that afternoon, my husband Matt came in from work, and said we were viewing a property the next day – it was the same house I had seen in the paper.

We have always been in sync with each other, not always having to speak words to communicate, more on a telepathic level. When we met, it was soul recognition, instant from the beginning. We were engaged within 6 weeks, married 14 months later, and have had 41 lovely years together. We have 7 beautiful children, one of them being a spirit son, which I will share with you later.

Life has not always been plain sailing, like many people, we have had a lot to deal with, but have always worked together and helped each other through everything. When one of us has been down, the other has stayed strong and helped pull them through. I believe this is the roots of a strong marriage.

The house was definitely calling us when we viewed it.

Within no time, we had an offer on our home and another accepted on Horton Vale Nursery. However, a few weeks down the line, it all fell apart, when our buyer withdrew. Horton Vale Nursery had four other buyers try to purchase it, but I kept saying to my husband it is waiting for us. My gut feeling was too strong to ignore.

My guides kept drawing my attention not to the beautiful house, but to the oldest building there. It was currently being used as their potting shed. I still don't know, if I was right, but it had the energy of once being used as a cattle shed. I had learnt to trust my guides completely and it was because of the strong feelings I had for this old building, I wanted to buy Horton Vale Nursery. This building was to become very important to us later, in more ways than one, as the years progressed.

My family and friends thought I was mad, when I told them it was the old building that was calling me and not the house which stood in its own garden on the four-acre site. However, as the years passed, everyone began to see why and for me, my faith in the guidance from my spiritual guides was proven yet again.

At this time, I would connect in with my guides and choose a tarot card to double check what was happening and more often than not, I was shown the Karmic Gift card. There are 78 cards in a tarot pack and when shuffled, if the same card keeps showing, it definitely needs to be listened to. So, I knew it would be a good move, but one we would learn from. This card often appears when the universe is trying to help you onto an important part of your pathway. However, there will be karma involved. You can pull a tarot card for guidance, but everything must be personal responsibility.

It was to be a year, before we received the keys for Horton Vale Nursery. This, however, gave us the time to spend with Matt's mum before she passed, without dealing with a house move on top. The universe knew exactly what it was doing and what was right for us.

As I have said before, I have always felt really looked after, even when times have been hard. Our guides never leave us, but we have come back to earth to learn certain lessons and the emotions attached to them. So, when life on earth feels difficult, such as deaths, births, house moves, divorce, redundancy etc., our guides are still very much around and supporting us, but will step back a little, to allow the transitions and learnings to develop. They will guide us back onto our spiritual pathways when the time is right if we take too long away. It is just a matter of having faith and trust, which can only be gained over time.

My guides always tell me, if someone is experiencing stress give them more and they won't have time to ponder on it.

Within weeks of the sale completing on our Grey Willows home, Matt's mum's family bungalow also sold. Moving two houses and two businesses was a venture we wouldn't want to repeat again. But on further reflection of the timescale of all this, it was actually perfect for our move forward once all the hecticness of the house moves had settled.

I love seeing the synchronicities in life and how everything happens for a reason at exactly the best time and will always be right for what we need.

'I have always been drawn to herbs, but not necessarily running a nursery so why would I even think of buying one!'

My guides started to show me, almost like premonitions, of how I could bring the animals, plants, and my spiritual work together as to me they were all part of a whole picture. Everything I had always enjoyed and worked hard at – I just had to find a way – but I had a dream.

Referring back to my influencing timeline and where my roots lay – When dad was young, his dad, my grandad, kept pigs, on a spare plot of land at the back of his garden. This brought meat for the family and local butcher, and he would go shooting for rabbits, pheasants, deer etc., They all had vegetable plots, it was a sign of the times to provide what was needed. I have lovely memories of spending time picking fruit with my cousins, in the orchard next door, bringing the bounty home and making jams, chutneys and puddings with mum. It was all part of life back then, with the teachings being passed forward. I would like to add that whilst so much of my heritage I have embraced, I still don't like the shooting of animals. I know life was far different after the war, it was part of survival, and we should not judge. It can be said that control is needed with wild animals, such as male deer and rabbits. However, after living in the country, most of my life, I have seen that nature has a very good way of sorting itself out.

One year we were inundated with wild rabbits. These are a food source for foxes, so it wasn't long before the foxes moved in and the rabbits became scarce, so the foxes moved back out again. Where there is a food source the animals will appear. They are no different than us in our search for survival. It's like mice and rats, will be more prolific around our outbuildings and animal sheds during the damp and winter months. However, when the crops start to grow in the fields, they move back out. The elements, cold winters, and droughts in the summer, also pay their own part.

I remember walking local, country hedgerows with mum, and our cream Labrador Barron, picking berries, chestnuts, hazelnuts and cockling in the sea when the tide was out at Sandbanks. So much of this, I carried through into my own life and work to help the animals and educate people. If you watch the birds, they stock up on the harvest of berries at the end of Summer, making their blood rich, to help them through the winter months. Hens will nibble the new shoots from the stinging nettles and cleavers as they come through at the start of Spring. They are very good for detoxing the body after its winter's storing time, which helped the body keep warm. If you pick the new nettle leaves, they don't sting, like the larger older ones.

There are many things to make from hedgerow and garden finds, all very beneficial to your health.

I felt life changed in the 80's, with the rise in convenience foods and fast pace of life. The natural ways of living seemed to be slipping away seemingly lost forever. So many from the younger generations were not shown how to cook, bake, sew, grow their own vegetables, keep poultry, grow their own fruit, and respect and learn lessons from Mother Nature, which is all around them. When we take the time to watch, we learn so much. Everything in life does eventually turn full circle and will come back again but in a different way as we all evolve and change.

My parents always grew their own plants and encouraged us to learn alongside them. There was always a vegetable plot and a greenhouse full of seedlings and cuttings, rhubarb growing out of old chimney pots to encourage the early growth, parsley ready to eat just after the winter months in the warmth of the greenhouse. Dad used to enjoy growing different types of Chrysanthemums, picking out some of the new buds to encourage bigger flowering heads on the remaining ones. The geranium summer bedding plants were always transplanted and brought into the home at the end of the summer months, for them to continue flowering throughout the whole of winter, providing an abundance of flowers in the home. Then around February time, cuttings would be taken for the summer hanging baskets. This way there were flowers all year round. Window boxes and planters adorned their home, filled with plants such as Swiss

Balcony Geraniums that would tumble down amongst the trailing fuchsias. There was always a mass of colour and competition to have the best hanging baskets. Flowers such as Dahlias were grown alongside different shrubs as mum loved her flowers and later trained in floristry. Sunflowers were grown for their seeds. Even weeds such as chickweed, dandelion heads, Plantain had a place as this was encouraged for dad's birds.

So, you see plants and animals have always been a very big part of my life.

Everyone used to have an Uncle Ted, and my dad was no exception. He was a twin and had a smallholding in Throop, Bournemouth. I remember dad taking me to visit as a child, there were rows and rows of vegetables growing. We would always come home with enough to last a couple of weeks. They were really good as well. He used to supply all the local shops.

It starts with patience, endurance, and a little understanding, before you start to hear tiny, very faint chipping, did you really hear it or was it your desire for it to happen? – after 21 days of waiting for the chicks to break out of their shells. No matter how many times I experienced seeing this, I would still marvel at how wonderful nature was. How could this little chick be created in a shell? Even how it was folded inside was a miracle in itself.

I loved sharing the hatching of the poultry eggs with our children, as my dad had done with me and his family with him. My grandad often kept poultry in large sheds, with artificial lighting to provide more daytime hours in the winter months, which would have helped increase the egg laying. The eggs being used for the family and sold to local people, as were the vegetables. This would possibly have been similar or the fore runner to the battery farms, we see as so wrong today. However, it also shows us how life has changed since the war and how far we have come to understand animals.

They were living in a time of surviving and providing for their families when everything was rationed and making work whatever resources they had around. I find it interesting that the same things go full circle, but we develop further with each cycle. Now we are seeing a rise in fresh, and home grown produce again. Farm shops are plenty as are the queues for allotments!

I mention this just because I found it interesting when I was told. My grandad was also a shoemaker, when the building work was quiet, he would repair footwear at a local shop. He crafted beautiful shoes with soles from different colours of leather. Dad recalls him cleaning his boots when he joined the army – 'shone so well, you could see your teeth in them,' he used to say. So, I have grafting in my genes and a passion for life and what it teaches us.

It was the year 2007 and the message from my guides strongly suggested it was a time for people to reconnect with herbs.

Horton Vale Nursery was a perennial nursery, with a lot of the plants being herbaceous. I have always kept everything as natural as possible for ourselves and our animals. Such as food and natural surroundings, together with chemical free products and herbs for wellbeing, so this was a good opportunity to explore it even further.

I grew herbs for the animals, not only for their general health, but also to help with mite, lice, worms etc., they can suffer with. It's interesting to note, that most of these herbs are perennials, growing through the warmer months, when the insects are rife and dying back through the winter when the insects aren't around. Most animals are very good at self-selecting herbs, as they would in the wild, and usually only take what they need. We talked to our customers about the different herbs to grow in their own gardens. Also, to rotate and use different ones, as I believe change is good.

Through my guides and spiritual awareness, I have been shown, we don't have to digest herbs to feel their effects. Their energies can interact with our auras and work on an energetic level. This means If you grow insect repellent herbs around plants and even animals the damaging insects won't come near, but pollination will still take place with other more necessary insects still playing their part. It can be the scent, colour, energy they emit etc., that enables this.

I love Basil in my kitchen, its smell, texture etc., but I don't enjoy eating it. I believe flowers carry their own vibrational healing energy and messages and it can be this that links with us. Such as primroses can sometimes call those who have rejected love, through their own misconstrued views of how it should really be. I always see Marjoram attracting those who need to release emotionally. I have planted Rue as a protector of my herb garden and Lavender at the entrance to our home for its energetic shield. So, you can start to see how I intended Horton Vale Nursery to work with the spiritual, plants and animals.

Whilst having a coffee with some friends, the name 'The Healing Garden Centre.' was born. It was channelled through to my friend Angela, whilst we were pondering on a name.

My husband and I worked lots of hours to make it happen. We extended and renovated the old potting shed for our work. Built a barn in which to hatch the poultry and house the nursery machinery, constructed chicken, duck, goose pens to accommodate our coups, Pigsties and strongly fenced areas, rabbit houses and runs. Plus, lots more. All designed so the animals could live as free range as possible.

At Horton Vale Nursery, we reared Kune-Kune pigs, but not for meat. All our piglets went to good homes. In the 1970's they were very close to extinction, with less than 2,000 in the whole world. So, it was good to be helping. They are also adorable and can become quite hand tame, even rolling over for their tummies to be rubbed. One of our pigs once had 16 babies, which is too many as they only have 12 nipples. We did try to hand rear, but this time it wasn't successful. When we were working in or around their pens, they would always come and lay near us. I loved hearing their grunts as they foraged in the dirt, coming up with muddy snouts.

We also kept the large French Lop Rabbits with their complimentary double chins. Beautiful rabbits in different colours, but I loved the blues and the reds. They made brilliant house rabbits, being very tame and also like little dogs.

I got used to our customers' comments, and I expect many of you have also had similar experiences, such as I didn't realise hens had different personalities, they have brought our garden alive, my children now eat eggs, and they love collecting them each morning. They provided something for families and elderly people to care for, to give them something to get up and do. As we bred them, quite a few went to care homes, holiday parks where the owners looked after them for others to see and enjoy and of course eat the freshly laid eggs. Some even went to schools to educate the young. Even the pigs went as pets or as rotavators to manure and turn over large vegetable plots, just as the Victorians used to use them.

I always wonder why more people didn't keep poultry. They are just as easy to look after as rabbits, guinea pigs, dogs, and cats, but they provide eggs, and you can't beat fresh eggs from happy hens. They carry good energy which when digested passes into your energy fields.

For some time, it was mainly people with land and farms that came and brought the hens, but my guides told me it wouldn't always be this way. I saw big changes coming when we moved to Horton Vale Nursery.

Then came the campaigns against battery hens and the poor-quality eggs they produced. More people began keeping their own poultry. I even started teaching chicken keeping workshops – each one full every time, which was lovely to see. It was through sharing this knowledge that gave me the courage to talk in larger groups. I know this was inspired by my guides never ending efforts to encourage me forward with my public speaking, in a way I was comfortable with – talking about the animals I had a passion for. It is from a lifetimes experience. I still continue to use this knowledge when teaching my animal healing and communication workshops.

Spirit will call my attention when there is a message to be given and I have learnt not to ignore it. The signs will become stronger and stronger and repeated until it's been delivered.

Looking at the smartly dressed lady in front of me at our nursery, her arms full of plants for her garden and dreams of how they were going to look in her flower beds, I knew she was totally unaware of my spiritual gifts. I wondered why spirit had to choose this moment to give me a message for her but knew they would keep repeating it until it had been delivered. Little did I know then this was to become a regular occurrence. There were two types of customers – your everyday down to earth gardener or family and others who knew all the Latin names and one could imagine regular trips to Chelsea Flower Show, with strong competition in growing the best plants. As you can imagine, the second type, were the ones I dreaded the messages coming through for. However, it was my earthly eyes seeing it this way.

My guides always show me on a soul level, we are all the same. You could be doing a reading or healing for the King of England and on a soul recognition level, he would be no different than you or me, with lessons to learn and different emotions to experience. Some of my customers still come for their healings and readings. Others learnt Reiki, crystal, and animal healing. Whilst others, I know from their reactions and facial expressions, the messages gave them great comfort at that moment in time.

Lewis Matthew our spirit son

Sitting in the ambulance watching the paramedic work endlessly to revive our little baby, I felt as though I was in another world or a parallel existence. Everything was going on around me, I could function, answer questions, but I felt like I wasn't there.

That morning had sent us all into total shock. The silent drive to the hospital was horrendous and lasted forever, whilst I had nothing to do but watch his little hand hanging lifeless over the side of the bed. My thoughts going back to my husband still at home, consoling and trying to explain to our two young daughters whilst coping with this himself.

This was a day that would change our lives forever. Lewis died from cot death at only 11 weeks old. He was so tiny, but it was enough time for him to come into our lives and turn them completely upside down, as all babies do.

He was a beautiful, blonde haired little soul, with dainty

features and was so good. I couldn't have asked for an easier baby.

'They often say only the good die young.'

Bank holiday Monday, 26th May 1987

I still remember the time he passed. Lewis only had a slight cold, but I felt worried. Was this justified or Mother's intuition?

I would normally ring my mum or sister to discuss whether to bother the doctor. However, this time, I just made an appointment with a locum, as our surgery was closed for the bank holiday. I was assured he was fine and to give him Calpol, if I felt he needed it. We then spent a lovely family day with my husband's dad. The weather was gorgeous over the whole weekend and my father-in-law took lots of photos of the children, which we will always be so grateful for, as little did we know Lewis was to be called back home, sometime during the night.

When I look back, I am sure my sudden visit to the doctor and being so out of character, was my sixth sense telling me something was wrong.

That morning, it was not the face of a loving dad looking at his baby son in his crib, that I could see, but one of devastation and shock. Why had Lewis not woken us with his early morning cry? The colour of his lifeless body confirmed our worst nightmare. His crib was right next to my bed, why had I not heard a thing? No parent expects to bury any of their children.

To me, a lot of this time is a blur and I believe the mind and body go into coping mode, to deal with the shock and stress. I do remember being so tired after this and just wanting to sleep. Whilst part of this can be not facing up to things, we do heal whilst in our sleep state.

I could see the family and funeral cars lining the street from my bedroom window, but I couldn't face leaving the house. My legs and thoughts just wouldn't coincide. This was a journey I really didn't want to take.

The white coffin was so tiny as it was gently carried down the church isle and I can't recall many of the people there, but the church was full and I am sure it was a lovely service, but I don't remember any of it.

My best friend Debbie had taken my daughters out somewhere nice. Being so young, they didn't need to experience the pain of the day. They had already seen enough. Lewis was laid to rest in the same graveyard as our grandparents, with an angel and these beautiful words on his gravestone:

'Those we love don't go away
They stay beside us everyday
Unseen, unheard but always near
The son we lost and loved so dear.'

One of the big regrets we both have, is the post-mortem showed no reason for his death. If it had been a bad heart, pneumonia, or anything it would have given us something to blame. To this day we still don't know the reason why, our beautiful baby went to sleep and never woke up.

'Nothing lasts for ever and sometimes we are not in control,
the universe will step in and bring change if needed.'

As I have already said, I have always been shown, that we choose our mums, dads, brothers, sisters, friends, and significant people we need to learn something from, before we reincarnate, to help us fulfil this lifetime's purpose. Everyone plays a part as do the different events and emotions we need to experience to progress our souls. So, losing our son would have been part of this. He only needed to be born and on the earth plane for those few weeks and his passing would have created different emotions for our family, grandparents, friends etc., to experience and learn from. Also, he only needed to be born and live those few weeks for the further development of his own soul. Everything, no matter what emotions it may bring, is always part of a much bigger picture.

I believe there is a set time for our birth and death. Sometimes, we will step off our pathway. However, if we stay away for too long our guides will try to bring us back onto our chosen route. They will never tell us what to do, everything is always personal responsibility.

It was strange after Lewis's death, how different people came into my life, who also ended up losing babies. One friend lost one of a twin: another a stillborn and someone else a miscarriage. All hard lessons in their own right and all little souls that returned home far too soon in our earthly eyes. The universe will always attract like with like and I believe these people were brought into my pathway, as I had already trodden this path and was able to truly help them. As I did this, it also aided my healing, it is often a two-way process. By saying this we will never ever forget Lewis, but somehow over time and I honestly don't know how or when, but we did start to look at life again and smile and laugh without feeling guilty.

We were elated when the following year, on exactly the same date as Lewis died – 26th May, our next daughter, Pettina was born. Lewis is always remembered, but it helped turn a very sad day into a happy one, with her birthday celebrations each year. Synchronicity at work again.

Here follows another beautiful poem a distant relative sent us at the time, which illustrates the dark times we go through, are just as important as the gold and silver threads of life to make up the colours of life's tapestry:

My life is but a weaving
Between the Lord and me
I may not choose the colours –
He knows what they should be.
For he can view the pattern
Upon the upper side
While I can see it only
On this, the under side
Sometimes he weaves in sorrow,
Which seems so strange to me,
But I will trust his judgement
And work on faithfully
Tis he who fills the shuttle
And he knows what is best
So, I shall weave in earnest
And leave to him the rest
Not till the loom is silent
And the shuttles cease to fly
Shall God unroll the canvas
And explain the reason why.
The dark threads are as needed
In the Weaver's skilful hand
As the threads of gold and silver
In the pattern, he has planned

By Corrie Ten Boom

We all perceive God or Lord as what we feel is right. For me I always see it as higher vibrational energy that encompasses Mother Earth, nature, spirit and far beyond, that shapes this world and our lives. This poem is a beautiful body of writing and was received with heartfelt gratitude.

I couldn't ignore or hate the little one sleeping contentedly in his car seat, placed at the other end of the room, so as not to inflict anymore pain on me or others. He was my nephew, born just 10 days before Lewis. My sister and I had gone through our pregnancies together. There were two ways of dealing with this. I knew which one I would take, as the other wasn't in my heart. I could resent my nephew for surviving or I could enjoy watching him grow, knowing that each milestone, special birthday, would be a reminder of the stage my son would have been.

Our minds are so powerful and if we try to keep positive, everything will eventually fall into place. It's not always easy, but if we replace a negative reaction or thought with a positive, it helps lift our vibrations and what we attract into our lives.

The day Lewis returned back home to the spirit world, changed everything for us as a family. Even to this day, the way our daughters respond to their children is a reflection from everything that happened at that time.

We are all a creation from our parents,' grandparents,' great grandparents' past, and the emotions experienced and taught forward.

When I am working with healing, we often look back at timelines and why our parents treated us like they did. It is often because they experienced certain emotions themselves when younger, that caused them to respond this way, which creates different lessons for us to learn and grow from. Sometimes this can be hard for us to understand.

After Lewis's death as parents, we were constantly, un-subconsciously, looking for the next breath from any sleeping baby. Each of our subsequent children were raised with breathing monitors, which would set off an alarm if they didn't breath within the set time. That day created a lot of fear. Subsequently, I now teach not to hold onto fear, or it will make you weak. When we step into our fears, we become strong. However, some are easier to release than others.

As I was struggling to let go of the fear that a sleeping baby could easily not wake up, the universe stepped in to help:

It was years later, when our first granddaughter Summer was about 10 weeks old, practically the same age as Lewis when he passed. My daughter and her husband had a friend's wedding to attend but could not take the baby. We never showed it but were secretly dreading the night. The same old thoughts of a sleeping baby not waking back up crept in. I decided if I had to stay up all night then so be it. However, this didn't happen, but it did help us overcome the fear we had held onto for far too long.

'When it is our time to return home, no matter what age, it will happen.'

As I mentioned before, like attracts like, and also different people come into our lives to help us through different situations.

I was only 19 when we married. My old needlework teacher from school, was helping me design and make my own wedding dress, when another lady named Jeanette joined the evening classes. It turned out I had gone to school with her younger sister. I was even more surprised, when we set our wedding date for 18th July, to discover Jeanette had also set her wedding for that very same day. We became good friends and the coincidences continued for some years. We never discussed any of this beforehand it just happened.

We both had our first daughters within a few weeks of each other in June and our second daughters approximately 16 months later in October. My next baby was our son Lewis, whom as you know passed back to the spirit world and she also had a little boy this time just after me, that was stillborn. We went on to have two more daughters, once again arriving around the same times. How weird was all of this and you couldn't have tried to make it happen as those of you who have babies know only too-well they arrive when they are ready.

Eventually, life started to take us on different pathways. It was a lovely, trusting, and supportive friendship that just fell into place, but the synchronicities were amazing.

Communications from
the Spirit World

Our guides will often use different elements to get our
attention, such as electricity and the flashing of lights,
T.V. interference, a telephone or doorbell ringing with no-
one there when answered, or water and the dripping of a tap,
which doesn't have a problem. My therapy room lights work
absolutely fine most of the time, but when I have a client and
they want to get a particular point across they have shown
me, the lights will flash until I deliver the message. Often
when words from a particular song are on my mind, when I
stop and review them, they are usually very significant. Once
I understand what they are showing me, or pass the message
on, the song disperses.

Adorning one wall in my therapy room are psychic
art pictures. Works of art hand drawn for me by different
spiritual artists. Some mediums work this way, instead of
doing a reading they will feel pulled to portray who they
see around or connecting in with you, which can often be a

guide or a loved one. Sometimes they will also give messages from them.

'Are they just artist's pictures hanging on a wall?'

It's like friends greeting me, when I walk into my treatment room and see the psychic art pictures of my guides and spirit son, which adorn one of the walls. They have been seen to change, even by surprised clients. My guides sometimes work with the energy from the picture, to prove they are around or have a message.

I was sure the face looking out at me from the picture, started to change, but when I took a second look it was still. I looked away trying to concentrate on something else, but my thoughts came back to the pictures hanging there. They were psychic art drawings created with intuitive energy, channelled through to the artist. Spirit energy. Drawn as a channel from the spirit form illustrated, to connect and guide the person drawn for.

'The energy within them never dies, as long as the person still believes.'

An Interesting Night's Work

The sea breeze was fresh, as it brushed against our central heated faces. So, invigorating after a busy night's work, as we walked back along the pathway, on the edge of Poole Quay in Dorset. The soft moonlight shone in all its glory, highlighting a silver pathway to our cars in the dark of the night. We were hyped up, after a satisfying spiritual evening's work at a local, charity psychic fair and were chatting excitedly. However, suddenly on hearing my friend's words, I stopped – "Lorraine there is an older lady sitting in the front seat of your car." For a brief moment, I thought she was referring to a physical lady and wondered why or how she had gotten there. However, on looking further, I could see the spirit form and instantly realised who it was. A lovely soul – Pat Joseph – the psychic artist who had drawn some of my pictures.

My thoughts reverted back to the start of my evening and the unusual happenings whilst at home …

Some years back, before Pat Joseph passed over, I was working at a spiritual event in a beautiful place called Bindon Abbey in Wool. It had once been a Cistercian monastery, built in 1172, with so much character and history. We were in a large top room, which spread the width of the building and had been recently refurbished exquisitely, using its history as a platform for the art decor. Just sitting in the quiet of that room was healing in itself.

Everything was set and perfectly ready for the day ahead. However, despite everyone's efforts the day was extremely quiet, with not many attending. Sometimes events can go like this, but it is always better to look at the bigger picture. My work schedule had been very busy, and I was tired. The spirit world knew I wouldn't just take time off, so had provided me with a day of rest, in a place where I would have no other option and what better place than within the beautiful relaxing, meditative energies of the Monastery.

As I sat there, I kept being drawn to an elderly lady opposite me and the colours in her artwork. That afternoon she connected with her guides, the spirit world around me and drew a psychic art picture of a young man with a cheeky smile, but I didn't feel any connection. She carefully rolled the artwork and gave it to me. After this day, it stayed stored in the back of my wardrobe until the strange happenings on the night of the Poole Quay Fair.

As I was getting dressed for the charity event, this picture somehow fell out from the back of the wardrobe. For the past few years, it had been safely stored high up on the top shelf. So why had it chosen to call my attention now?

As I grabbed everything together for the evening, a leaflet fell onto the floor – it was Pat Joseph's the psychic artists – I didn't even know I had it. So, when I saw her spirit form in the front of my car, I knew I had to look more closely. What was Pat trying to show me?

That night when my home was quiet, I asked my guide to help me understand what was being shown. As I unrolled the picture, it connected with me. Although it was of a young man and my son passed when a baby, I saw the same round cheeks he had, and I will never forget. That cheeky smile in the picture was beginning to talk to me.

My spirit son has always given so much proof he is around, which I will talk about later, but he had grown in the spirit world.

My guide has told me he was an old soul that didn't need to stay on the earth plane for long. His birth and early death were another experience for his growth and spiritual development, to help him fulfil his contract so to speak, for this lifetime. He only needed to experience the birth, the few weeks he was here, and his death created emotional growth for those around him to learn from.

I now had a psychic art picture of him. When I looked closer, I could see the resemblance to my other son, his brother.

Many who view this picture, see a Tibetan Monk, so it was extra special my guides chose to gift this to me whilst at the Monastery.

I remember questioning my guide, as to why my son appeared to me as older and highly evolved. I was shown when babies pass over, they continue to grow, to an age where they would have been at the prime of their life. The same as when elderly people return home to the spirit world, often after suffering illness, they will also revert back to a younger age, when they were their strongest or happiest, with the illness gone. Any diseases or physical disabilities are only needed in this lifetime, for the emotions they cause and to be learnt from. Whilst extremely upsetting and something I would hate to go through again – the loss of a child, I know it was for a special reason, why we were chosen to be Lewis's parents. He only needed to be conceived, born and to live for those few 11 weeks to develop what he needed on a soul level, and he taught us a lot.

I have been shown spirit children are looked after by grandparents or loved ones from the earth plane and also spirits who never had the chance of childhood on earth. They are highly skilled and love their job. The spirit children continue to develop and are taught spiritual insights and lessons, not as we are taught on the physical plane. They are never alone and will stay still connected to their earth parents until it is their time to return to the spirit world, as their bond of love cannot be broken.

I would just like to add, I would not be working as I do today if Lewis's death had not happened. As I said before, we need to have trodden the pathway ourselves to be able to fully help others.

Lewis has given us so much proof that he is around, and I share just some of them below:

Night-time had fallen once again, with all the children asleep and tucked up neatly in their beds. The whole house was now in sleeping mode and a tranquil vibration could almost be heard oscillating around the whole of the house, with just a quiet noise from the television echoing from the lounge. The house put back into order again, washing up done and tidied away, last wash put on, followed by that gorgeous feeling as you eventually fall onto the settee, knowing your day's work has been done and at last it's your time. Your whole body begins to relax as all the aches and pains of a busy day just begin to melt away, when you hear those little footsteps run right across the landing.

Those with children will know what this feels like only too well.

However, as I climbed the stairs to put the escapee back into bed, I went from room to room only to see all the little ones still fast asleep. Had I been hearing things? were they pretending? No, their sleep was too deep.

I retreated downstairs again to nestle back into my own time, when the same footsteps ran back across the landing – my spirit son was making himself known, running between the children's rooms, and visiting them in their dream states.

We were excited to be moving into our newly built home with all the furniture and furnishings fitting into place. High up above the fireplace was an aged oak beam where I evenly placed photos of my 6 children. With any O.C.D I had kicking in they were evenly positioned; I had made sure of that before I went into a different room to complete another task.

I kept thinking at this time about my spirit son. Was it because I had been getting pictures out of the others? I really didn't know, but I suddenly had such a strong inclination to include a photograph of Lewis. I only had one of suitable size as he had passed so young. When I went back into the lounge and looked up at the other pictures I had evenly placed on the beam – they had definitely moved. Lewis was baby number three and there was now a large gap between my first two daughter's pictures and number four so to speak, making enough room for another picture frame. It was amazing to see. The beam was far too high for any of the children to reach and my husband was busy with another job. My guide confirmed Lewis wanted to be included with the other children in our new home, another beautiful connection and proof from the spirit world.

At the end of the main hallway, was an airing cupboard with double doors. So why did some days the doors stay completely closed and others no matter how many times you shut them, they would be open the next time you looked or passed by?

What was that tingling feeling in the back of my head? I would scratch it, but when I did there was no itch there, in fact no feeling at all. As you know, when you have an itch, the relief you get from scratching that area, is lovely. It was a vibrational energy that came only at certain times on the back of my head. But why was I getting it?

I needed to work out what was going on and after contemplation, I was intuitively shown to watch what good news, events, different emotions etc., came during the day or week when these things happened. It was my spirit son again, trying to get my attention when there was something major or exciting about to happen, such as a new baby, a birthday, someone visiting, etc., etc., since his passing he has definitely let us know, he is around to help and support us all.

Referring back to the airing cupboard door, which was some years ago now, my husband found it hard to believe it was our spirit son and passed it off with a more physical explanation. He went about placing more secure locks, and he always does everything properly and definitely not by halves – the door still opened at relevant times.

When spirit connects, it can feel like a soft vibrational energy or tingling. We have to remember they no longer have a physical body and are just vibrational energy. They can link in with our auras, to manifest and show themselves, to prove they are around. However, this takes a lot of effort, and they also have to learn how to do it. When spirit is around, we can also see orbs of energy, little flashes of light or feel extremely cold. Sometimes I can sense a slight vibration across the width of my shoulders, which I now know is my gran, when she draws near and places her arm around me.

'So how did my spiritual journey start? That's a very good question.'

As a child, lying in bed at night in the upstairs bedroom I shared with my sister, I just knew we weren't alone and felt like we were being watched.

During the night, I would run as fast as I could past the stairwell, to reach my parents' bedroom and once in their bed, I could hide away from the constant stares and the feeling of being surrounded by others that weren't in a physical form. My dad always said, to his last days, if he put me back to bed once, he would put me back loads of times, I just didn't like it in that room. Now, I realise maybe it wasn't the room, but the constant presence of something I didn't fully understand at that time. I always felt I was being looked after, but I didn't want it or like it.

I could hear the clanging of the hand rung school bell as I was just reaching the school gate. A daily occurrence of running through the entrance at the last minute and arriving just on time, under the watchful glare of the headteacher, who used to stand at the school gate.

This, in the nick of time behaviour, was a possible bad habit I still carry through today.

I remember being young and writing in pencil and it seemed to take weeks before I accomplished neat handwritten skills, and a piece of my writing was good enough to be displayed on the classroom wall.

This was probably as I like to print but had to show the constant flow of my pen into joined up writing is something else, I still very rarely do today. However, I loved school and the learnings it gave me, and I really should have gone into teaching when I left college. I did well at school, became a prefect and nearly head girl. I loved netball, played for the school team, learnt to play the recorder, guitar, and trumpet, and enjoyed helping run the school bank which was set up to teach pupils about money and saving. I left school with what was then, good exam results. College followed and I qualified as a shorthand, audio typist and worked as a secretary for National Westminster Bank. However, on looking back at my favourite times I remember art, needlework, baking, and netball all creative activities and how much I hated maths.

Little did I realise back then that the conversations in the school playground and later in life discussions in the work staffroom was me using my intuition and part of my biggest spiritual gift coming into play.

People have always felt safe to talk with me and unload their problems. Even as a child I remember seeing the answers so clearly, but also thinking that was so easy, why couldn't they work it out for themselves. At such a young age, I didn't realise, I was using my spiritual gifts, clairsentience, clairaudience, and clairvoyance with my intuition. I was too young and inexperienced to realise, this was the first signs of my pathway as a healer. I could feel and see their emotions and pain, but also the way through it. This is something that has carried on throughout my life and I still work this way today with my clients. Often someone will come into your life, just at the right time to help you through a certain situation, but we don't always recognise it.

We all have our own journeys, but we can't always see the solutions to our own problems. If we could, we would never learn the lessons that go with them. If you look back over your own lives, you will recall that life is full of ups and downs, with good and bad times. We need hard and challenging times in life to appreciate the good. It often runs in 3-, 5- or 7-year cycles. So, you could have 5 good years followed by 5 difficult. However, it is through the tough times we learn, grow, and become stronger. It is also life often pushing us onto a different pathway or direction, because without our realisation and sometimes with reluctance, we have outgrown the present one.

I recall my dad always saying when I was struggling with something – the time to worry, isn't when you're down, as the only way is up, but when things are going well, make sure you use that time wisely and make provisions, as it will change, and things may not be so good. This was never meant as pessimistic, it was said with wisdom.

Have you ever witnessed a strong wind, blowing so profusely, and moving anything in its pathway, then suddenly for no unseeable reason at all it changes, becoming as light as a feather and gently blowing in a totally different direction? Well, this could also be a way of describing major life changes.

You know only too well those days when the sun is shining, the visor is pulled right down to shade your blinking eyes and you have an intense feeling of warmth and cosiness as you are driving through a country lane, and your thoughts begin to wander. Just why did I keep hearing the name Reiki in my mind's eye? Each time the words would echo in my head, I felt excitement and an intense feeling of knowing I was going to be doing it and felt very proud. But I didn't even know what it was. Was it just that I liked the sound of the unusual word. I really didn't know, but I did know it was something I was going to embrace, but did I really? Little did I realise then, my guides were directing me onto a major turning point on my pathway, which was going to become a very big part of my life. It has definitely been something I am extremely proud to have learnt and helped so many onto their Reiki journeys of transforming and understand their lives.

So, it starts as a dream,
And for a while is all it will seem,
But follow its light,
Allow those thoughts to shine bright,
Open your heart and allow it to sing.
You'll be surprised what abundance this will bring –
Happiness, strength, friends, and achievements
Change of direction and seeing life different
And it all started from just a dream.

By Lorraine Tricksey

There came a time

I truly wanted to understand my gifts, why did I have them and what was I to do with them? I was guided to join a spiritual development circle. I absolutely loved going and meeting other like-minded people and was beginning to develop a way forward with my readings and mediumship. However, spirit have a wonderful way of changing things, when we need to take the next step of our pathways and not always at the time, we would have chosen it to happen. I was so disappointed when the group leader decided to turn the development circle into a healing group. I had been told many times I was a healer, but in my mind, it wasn't at all where I was heading and at this time in my life, I didn't really know what an energy healer was.

How could you heal anyone by simply placing your hands on them? I almost felt a bit of a fraud or an idiot doing it. But I loved going to this group and really trusted and enjoyed the company of the people so decided to continue, telling myself, I would only take in that which made sense or was proven to me.

Little did I know what effect simply placing your hands on someone and working with your healing guides and the universal energies would have. My hands went extremely hot, I was guided to places and areas of pain or deep-seated emotions, I felt blocked energy that I wanted to clear. My development side kicked in with my healing and was intuitively guided to areas of dis-ease, sometimes, being shown childhood problems or past lives linked to the pain. Their physical bodies started to talk to me with their emotional symptoms and I was more often than not, shown the root cause and from there we started to move forward on their healing journey.

I soon discovered that it is important to keep your energetic body (aura) balanced as well as your physical body in good health. This is why it is good to work in conjunction with your general practitioner and holistic therapist. This can help keep your mind, body, and soul in balance.

Nowadays I have my own private practice and whilst some people may come for just one healing, as that is all that is needed, others require more sessions, depending on how deep seated the symptoms are in the energetic body. I love to see people grow in themselves becoming much stronger as they come to the end of their healing sessions. I am always shown when the sittings are coming to an end, as the energy will withdraw, coupled with a strong feeling of bringing them to a close.

In my training days, I remember when I was doing a healing session on a lady and was somewhat shocked when her leg shot up in the air, nearly hitting my nose and sent me into a fit of giggles. This was obviously blocked energy being released. At the beginning of my healing journey, as I have already said, I needed proof healing really worked, so at the start of each session, I would ask for it and every time spirit definitely provided. Sometimes I would feel absolutely nothing at all from my hands, no heat, cold or tingling, but at the end of the healing session the client would say oh gosh, I felt this and that ... and I remember thinking in my mind, thank goodness for that because I felt nothing, but I got to learn this does occasionally happen and even if we feel nothing the healing will still be working, and will transpire in ways we least expect. Nowadays, I have seen so much and sometimes it has felt like a miracle has happened, consequently I trust it fully, knowing it will always work for the client's highest good.

To truly understand, it is helpful if we have trodden the pathway ourselves and experienced similar situations. As we heal, others with similar emotions will be drawn to us. As we help them, we can also help ourselves. It's the universal law of attraction. You will often find that most mediums and healers have had quite hard lives.

'Our lessons give us the tools for our trade.'

My dad, the first great teacher in my life, spoke about memories of when his brother Alfie had been lost at war. I think the ship he was on had gone down, with little chance of survivors. My grandad told dad about a dream where he saw Alfie walking across the upstairs hallway. Now that could have been my uncle's spirit showing itself if he had passed over, but grandad was adamant about his feelings at this time and was sure Alfie was coming home and would walk back along that corridor. Some weeks later it happened, he had been injured, but came home.

So, you see spiritual gifts were actually in both sides of my family, although some lay more latent than others.

Many years later when I was setting up and running The Healing Garden Centre this grandad who passed when I was about five or six, would often connect in to help and guide me, being seen by other visiting mediums. In days gone by, to be spiritually wise wasn't often talked about. In fact, it was kept quiet because of the traits from the past, when many were hung, drowned, or even stoned. However, nowadays things have changed so much. and the wise old ways are actually embraced. The change has come in even more over the past twenty or so years. It is now, rarer, for someone to have never had a tarot reading or healing whereas before it was the other way around.

The story of my grandfather taught me a valuable lesson to always trust what your guides show you. It's a valuable point I still teach my students today. TRUST – If you feel, sense, or see something it is for a reason always trust your senses, they won't show you wrong. If you are feeling a certain way about a situation or a person, it will always be for a reason. Even if others say you are wrong. The more you trust your connections with yourself and the spirit world, the stronger the connections will get. Your intuition will never lie or let you down. My guides have always helped and enhanced my life especially in times of need and through my work helping others. When you work with spirit, if you put in 25%, they will add 75% as long as you are working from the heart and for the right reason.

All the lights had gone out and the house was once again quiet. I was five or six years old and thinking about life and death. It was probably the death of my grandad that initiated the thoughts, but I pondered on the sense of this. How we were ever created into this life was a miracle in itself. I thought of how hard dad worked to provide for us, the things different scientists created, the different friendships formed, families and even nature with its wonders, to then just die and be gone? It just didn't make sense. All that effort and creation would have been for nothing.

So, I have always had this search for knowledge and to understand life. To this day, it never ceases to amaze me how everything happens for a reason, at the right time, the right place and each happening tells a story and leads further into the universal plan. Quite often we can feel the timing is wrong, but when the bigger picture evolves reflection can prove different.

One of my spiritual gifts is clairaudience. How it works for me, is that it can come like thoughts that aren't my own spoken in my mind. Sometimes, I hear significant words or sentences when I am doing a reading or healing, but they will always be key important words which when enlarged on, help clients and those around me. The spoken words are not in my voice and always come into my thoughts on my right side. Most mediums cannot tolerate a lot of noise around them, as they have this constant talking going on in their heads.

I remember as a young child one of these such conversations. It was Christmas Day, and I was with my family happily unwrapping our gifts. My brother, who I have always been very close to un-wrapped a bike. I don't even remember looking at the bike, its colour, shape, or anything, I was too absorbed in my own presents, but the words just came from my mouth – that's my old bike sprayed up. It wasn't until I saw the look on my parents' faces, I realised what I had actually said and the shock I felt, at being right. What surprised me the most, was that the words hadn't even entered my head, they had just come from my mouth. I think I was just as shocked as them. To this day I have always regretted these words because who did they help? However nowadays, I know that everything happens for a reason and there were learnings from this.

We were in the middle of Bournemouth square, and it was buzzing with shoppers. Definitely a time when we were following our hearts and not our heads. We had only known each other 6 weeks but had decided to get engaged. A whirlwind romance, but just needed to tell our parents. I was 18 and Matt was 21. That gut feeling was showing itself again, and it felt right.

The night was busy, the music was loud, and the club was full. I normally loved Saturday nights out with my best friend Debbie, but that night I felt bored.

Looking around, I remember feeling annoyed at the men stood around the edge of the dance floor, watching the ladies dancing and it felt like a cattle market.

We left early intending to go home but stopped at a wine bar called 'Sour Grapes,' on the top of the Triangle. There was a long queue and as we got to the door, there was a sign saying, 'couples only,' so, we paired up with the couple of men in front of us, just to get through the door. Once inside, they brought us a drink to say thank you and history is the rest. This was how Matt and I met and 41 years later we are still together.

'When it's time for two souls to meet there is nothing on earth that can prevent them from meeting.'

However, going back to that day in Bournemouth Town Square, I recall another time of words being spoken without the thought form entering my head. We had just agreed to get engaged, but I was pondering over the fact, I hadn't even met Matt's family and it was strange he didn't seem to want me to. Matt had met mine and would speak lovingly of his family, but never talked of meeting them. I was about to ask why, when suddenly the words came out – 'your parents are divorced aren't they?' Once again, these words had been channelled through me.

It was instant as soon as we met. I believe that when two people meet on a soul level the connection is there and will not be broken until their souls' journeys and lessons have been seen through. My guides have also shown me, we have had many lives together.

Once I was teaching a workshop to a group of people and one particular lady kept calling my attention. Every time I looked at her, I was drawn to a black mass I was seeing in her right eye. When looking on a physical everyday level, I could see her eye as ordinary as anyone else's, but as I was tuned in for the workshop, I kept being shown this black mass. I started to have a conversation in my mind with my guides who were showing me this. There was no way I could give this to the lady as I was not a doctor, and I did not want to scare her. However, I knew, that if I was getting this message, it was for a reason, and I could not ignore it. Whilst teaching I was mentally saying to my guide you need to show me another way of delivering this message. When suddenly the words came from my mouth without entering my head again – you need to go and see an optician. I was so thankful and remember thinking what a brilliant way of saying it – they had helped me deliver the message in a way that was acceptable and if she took the advice given would be guided to the right professionals for help. Luckily, she did and from my experience with working further with this lady it has been one of the journeys that has made me believe in miracles with healing.

This lady went to her optician, and they confirmed seeing a black mass in the back of her eye, she was then put under a specialist at the hospital to work further with the problem. However, she also came to see me for healing. It was a terrific experience working with her and as well as the healing, the spirit world gave some lovely advice even to do with certain foods and lifestyle which were needed for the wellness of her body, working with the emotions attached to this problem and more. The lady followed everything through and continued to work with the specialists at the hospital. It took a few healing sessions, but it was wonderful when she came one day and said she had been for her hospital appointment and they had to call in another more experienced specialist to take a second look as they could not fully understand it, but where the black mass had been there was now scarring. It also showed me how when the medical profession and healers work together great results can be achieved. The medical profession, often work with the symptoms and healers work with the route cause, which usually have emotions attached to it.

I do believe in miracles and have experienced a few wonderful happenings in my time as a healer. However, I believe that we come back to learn certain emotions, and these will be repeated a few times in our lives, but in different ways, until we learn the lessons attached to them. If we don't deal with the emotions that really affect us, they start to ripple into our auric field (energy field) right at the tip of it and if we still do not heal them, they will ripple into our energy field until they hit the physical body and then this can result in illness or physical pain. They can still be healed at this level, but it is often much harder.

I believe miracles can only happen when we learn the lesson attached to these emotions and really let it go and change our ways. The illness can be seen to leave, however if we then fall back into the old ways, a bit like putting on an old pair of slippers, it can come back again, or a different illness will come in.

It's interesting to note that any illnesses or disabilities leave the soul when they pass back to the spirit world. They are only for their life's lessons whilst on the earth plane and when they return back home the souls often go back to the age when they were in the prime of their life.

I worked with a lady for over 12 years. She originally came to see me when her husband died unexpectedly and like so many others it was more than she could cope with. She had a beautiful kind, caring soul and worked as a local carer. However, I always saw her as a nurse in past lives, especially attached to the air force and would often see her in uniform in one of those lifetimes. She went through a terrible time loosing other people in her family who were also very close to her. She was always smiling even though her auric field showed different, and this was a lesson in itself for her to come for help, she was far better at giving it, but she would leave far more uplifted, rebalanced, and helped. Her dear husband was such a great support from the spirit world, and he had a very large energy and would always come through with evidence of some kind which definitely gave her support in her last years.

Some clients become more like friends, she was one and I was devastated when she came for another healing session some years later and told me she had liver failure and would need a liver transplant. We worked with spiritual healing and crystals and the emotions attached to illnesses of the liver and they all made sense. Like we can detox our livers and bodies through diet, we also need to detox our livers from stored emotions on an energetic level. So, when I am doing healing, I often work to remove blocked, stagnant energies from these areas which are also in our emotional area – the Solar Plexus.

She was a very sensible, logical lady with a good mind, and she trusted me completely because of the evidence, times of healing and teaching we had spent together, with the trust being built in these special times and I always work with my guides and from my heart to help others. However, I was completely shocked when she said to me, you have said I will not die from this illness. Now I knew I would never, ever have said this as it is in the healers' code of conduct and in my own ethics that we must not diagnose illnesses or predict cures, unless you are a qualified doctor. It left me in quite a predicament, and I felt that if I was to correct this and take away this thought form she had created, it would take away the hope from her mind. Whenever she said it, which was quite a few times I just listened, as through my work I know how powerful our minds can be. I have seen people diagnosed with different medical conditions by the hospitals and within days their whole constitution has gone downhill, and the illness has taken grip and changed their lives. So, I never agreed with her or took it away, I just surrendered it up to the universe to guide and help us both.

She came for regular healing sessions especially my monthly Reiki Share groups where at each session I took the group through a healing meditation and then they were all given chance to receive and give healing. The healers who come regularly to these sessions grow so much in their healing abilities and knowledge and they are always very enjoyable evenings.

> *'As a healer, it is always important to keep your own energy fields balanced to give balanced and good healings.'*

Sometimes she would arrive looking quite pale, tired. and not at all well and it was great for the other healers to experience and feel how her body absorbed the healing energies and after the session she would look like a different person. Many times, we did group healing sessions around her, which are very powerful ways of working. She walked out differently than she walked in and some of the healers often still comment on these experiences now.

During these times, she visited the specialists as well as working with the healing, but she never had the liver transplant, and she was excited to tell me how her medication had been reduced right down. In fact, she was so pleased to tell me the specialists were not sure why this was happening, and she would say it is Reiki healing helping me. Apparently, they would just reply, well whatever it is just keep doing what you are doing as it is obviously working.

Unfortunately, one evening she arrived with a scarf

around her neck, and she showed me a massive lump it was hiding. I felt sick because it was visually the same size lump in the same area, I had seen in another close friend of my husbands a few months before when he had been diagnosed with cancer. Tests later confirmed that she had cancer of the thyroid which had travelled down to her lungs and a few months later she passed over.

Reflecting back, I was pleased I hadn't taken away her thoughts about liver cancer not being the cause of her death, as she had been right it didn't cause it.

I believe we have pre-chosen times for us to reincarnate, with the time we are born, when we are due back home and the different experiences our soul needs to learn before this happens all set-in place. We will be guided and helped every step of the way, but never told what to do. We all have personal responsibility, but nothing is ever wrong as even if we do step from our chosen pathway we will learn from the journey. As long as we don't procrastinate for too long, we will come back onto our pathways and continue along our journeys older and wiser for the experiences. However, if we stagnate too long, we could miss out on key elements we have come back to learn, as I do believe there is a certain timescale for things to happen. When I say stagnate, this can often happen as when we are not going in the right direction and change is imminent, we can begin to feel quite blocked and it can seem like life is really hard, can even make us loose our inner sparkle. Life can sometimes be like putting on an old pair of slippers. The future can be scary as we don't know what it holds, so we often slip back into those old slippers as it is what we know, no matter how bad life is. However, if we step forward and embrace the new beginnings, sometimes blindly and often having to step into a fear, life will start to kick into place and take us to new experiences and the pathway we are meant to be on.

When my other son was 16, I knew it was important and a big part of his growing up and independence, as we lived in a rural area, for him to have a moped. I guess the same old fear of losing another son showed up. However, I was intuitively shown that if it was his time to pass or he was to be knocked off and hurt it would happen in some other way as it would be a part of his journey and even if I stopped it this way it would happen another, I didn't need to put my fears onto him. He did get a moped and apart from a small fall he was absolutely fine and grew so much from the experience.

> *'We should never lead our lives through fear.*
> *If we hold onto fear, it makes us weak.*
> *If we step into and embrace fear, it makes us strong.'*

We will always remember the way he tooted its horn without fail every time he came in and went out. It was so significant even our African Grey parrot copied it, so in the end we didn't know if it was Ashley coming home or the bird calling.

I hope you have enjoyed the teachings from my inward journey towards spiritual enlightenment and it also helps with your soul's pathway too.

I leave you with a thought-provoking poem channelled through to me:

> **'We should always do things in life to the best of our capabilities.'**
> We all need to try hard
> No matter what we do.
> If failure is experienced
> The one to blame is you.
> Put experience in your vocabulary
> To become as wise as can be.
> Life is your big playground
> Can you now See?
> Life isn't hard and doesn't need to be.
> If life is difficult, its only your view.
> So, re-look your journey and start again anew.
>
> By Lorraine Tricksey

I will also share with you a channelled message my guide came through to me with, as I expect you will also feel its significance:

Try to remember our ways are teaching pathways forward for the next generations. We are their teachers. Embrace enlightenment. You have had a lifetime of feeling out in the cold, maybe as though you don't belong, shouldn't have, don't deserve all possible negative concoctions which basically have no validation in your be-little'd soul. You have stretched up far and wide, travelled here and there in search for enlightenment and understanding of all the hardships in your life when the answer has always been buried deep within your soul. The time is right now for you to reach very deep from within and find the hidden treasure YOU have kept hidden from the world to see. A heart that is so pure and fair but with fear of being hurt. But you have kept it pristine as it was a treasure of yours. I see a perfect, absolutely perfect, bright red heart now ready to be shown to the world. BUT one that is strong and unfearful of being hurt and won't be because no soul of lower vibration will dare to come near because of the energy it vibrates. This is the true heart of a warrior, oh so strong who has fought now for way too long. Your body is weary, your sight has dwindled to give you only one capacity but to bear your heart. It is time to rise now my dear child your work is done and become a child again but a happy one. Let go of your past this journey is done and step forward again as a little one.

Passion, enthusiasm, love. and attainment are the only words that need to be searched as you have reached your own personal enlightenment. I see all the coldness of your past melting away and revealing a soul so pure and absolutely full of love no mountain will ever be too high as you have already climbed them.

To find out more about Lorraine Tricksey and her spiritual path, teachings, and healings, you can connect with her ...

www.Lorrainetricksey.com
Facebook... The Home Of Hocus Pocus
Instagram... thehomeofhocuspocus

This book is printed on paper from sustainable sources managed under the Forest Stewardship Council (FSC) scheme.

It has been printed in the UK to reduce transportation miles and their impact upon the environment.

For every new title that Matador publishes, we plant a tree to offset CO_2, partnering with the More Trees scheme.

For more about how Matador offsets its environmental impact, see www.troubador.co.uk/about/